TRUE CRIME

Reader's
Digest

New York, NY / Montreal

CONTENTS

INTRODUCTION

What turns a seemingly ordinary person into a cold-blooded killer? What makes some people lie, cheat, and steal to get what they want, while the vast majority of us play by life's rules? This glimpse into the shadowy side of human nature is one reason true crime stories are inherently compelling. We're fascinated and repelled by the best criminal minds, so brilliant yet so twisted.

But true crime tales aren't only about the heart of darkness. We want to see good triumph over evil, especially in real life. Thus, we're also fascinated by clever and courageous crime fighters. What's it like to be an FBI profiler or an undercover detective? How do they get inside a criminal's head? And what about situations where crimes are stopped by just plain folks? What makes an average Joe or Josephine suddenly turn hero when observing wrongdoing? What makes a witness take the risk to become part of the process? And ultimately, what does it take to crack the case?

So many questions.

In their search for answers, true crime stories make for great reading. Over the years, *Reader's Digest* has covered true crimes both large and small, and *True Crime* has them all: petty theft, serial killers, lottery scams, kidnappers, art heists, and, of course, the granddaddy of them all: crimes of passion. These 24 tales of murder and mayhem are guaranteed to surprise, shock, and fascinate as they offer a glimpse into the twisted minds of criminals and the dedicated crime fighters who catch them.

TRUE
CRIME

A KILLER IS LOOSE

by Joseph P. Blank

As the residents of Jerseyville, a town of 7500 people in southwestern Illinois, started about their daily affairs on the mild, sunny Friday morning of October 9, 1969, alarming news wildfired among them: A cold-blooded killer was hiding somewhere in their area.

The twenty-one-year-old killer, James Gordon Palmer, was a Jerseyville man. Police Chief Herman Blackorby described him as "a nice-looking, nice-talking boy who didn't mind killing you." In a ramble through Missouri, Illinois and Tennessee he had robbed and murdered a bait-shop owner, a young waitress and a filling-station attendant. He had fired bullets into the backs of their heads—in the case of two of them, while they lay facedown on the floor—until they stopped moving.

On the night of October 8, sheriff's deputies had spotted Palmer as he drove up to his Jerseyville apartment. He raced them to the outskirts of town, jumped from his car and escaped the cornfield. An hour later he shot and wounded a railroad brakeman shining a lantern near a ditch where he lay hidden.

Now more than a hundred police, state troopers and sheriff's deputies had converged on Jerseyville. They put bloodhounds around the spot where Palmer had fled, but the dogs couldn't pick up a scent. They patrolled all roads and searched

hundreds of buildings. Each school bus carried an armed policeman. A helicopter and four small planes kept crisscross-
ing nearby farmlands. Radio broadcasters warned listeners to
lock their doors. Police feared that Palmer might massacre an
isolated farm family to steal a car. As the hours passed, the
people of Jerseyville grew increasingly jumpy. By afternoon
sporting-goods stores had sold out their supplies of guns and
ammunition. Several farm families drove into town to stay at
the hotel. One woman, hearing a noise in the basement, rid-
dled her kitchen floor with buckshot.

In the squat brick building that housed the two office
rooms of Gorman Brothers' Construction Company on Frank-
lin Street, business continued as usual. But that evening Louis
Gorman found his wife and two children frightened. Gorman, a
quiet and gentle man, fifty-two and graying, tried to reassure
them. "Palmer is probably well on his way to Mexico by now,"
he said.

Nevertheless, he slept restlessly. He arose before five,
dressed and drove down to Sandy's Café, where he drank
coffee and talked with two men from a posse that had searched
for Palmer through the night. Then, shortly after seven, Gorman drove to the office. Two truck drivers, Charles Kroeschel
and his son-in-law, Robert Cordes, arrived at the same time.

When Gorman put his key into the lock, he found it unlocked. He made a mental note to remind his men to check the
doors before leaving at night. Entering the building, Gorman
went to the washroom. He saw that the glass pane in the rear
door had been broken and covered with cardboard, but he assumed that one of his men had broken the window on the previous day. Meanwhile, Charlie Kroeschel walked around the
counter in the outer office, stepped into the inner office—and
was confronted by a man pointing a .22-caliber semiautomatic

rifle. Kroeschel's mouth fell open. He backed away, repeating incredulously, "Louie, he's here. That guy is *here*."

Palmer, tall, lean, blond, with a boyish face, said, "Do as I tell you and you won't get killed. Sit down on the floor of the inside office and don't move." Kroeschel and Cordes obeyed.

Gorman, in the washroom, heard Kroeschel's astonished words. Quickly he opened the washroom window, but he couldn't push out the screen. Palmer banged on the door and said, "Are you coming out or will I have to shoot you through the door?" Gorman came out.

"Sit down with your buddies," Palmer directed, the asked the trio if the owner of the business was among them. Gorman answered. The killer nodded toward him and said, "Open the safe, brother."

"I can't," Gorman said. "It's a tricky combination lock, and our office manager, Ernie Pohlman, is the only one who knows how to open it."

"Brother, you're lying," Palmer said evenly. "I've got a notion to kill you right now." He moved his rifle.

"I'm not lying. Ernie will open the safe when he comes in." Gorman later admitted he was scared. He had no way of knowing at what point a twisted whim might prompt the killer to start shooting.

At that moment truck driver Edward Fitzgibbons drove his pickup to the back of the building. Palmer crouched behind the service counter. Fitzgibbons, noticing the broken pane in the rear door, ambled into the office saying, "Hey, it looks like somebody broke in here."

Palmer rose from behind the counter, his gun leveled.

"And I'm still here," he announced. "You just sit down on the floor there with your buddies." Fitzgibbons did so.

The next captive was William Kuehnel, a railroad engineer

for the local freight line, who dropped in to tell Gorman that a car of cement had arrived. The engineer was followed by Herschel Andrews, a construction-equipment officer, and then truck driver Darrell Smith.

Ernie Pohlman was a little late that morning. Reluctant to leave his wife and three children in the house six miles out in the country, he had stayed to show his wife how to fire his shotgun. His first sensation when confronted by Palmer was relief: At least he knew his family was safe.

When Pohlman identified himself, Palmer said, "Just the man. Open the safe, Ernie."

Pohlman knelt before the safe, which for a long time had been difficult to open. He twirled the knob. He failed on the first try. He failed again. In a warning tone Palmer said, "Ernie!" Again Pohlman muffed the combination. Palmer said, "Ernie, I'll give you one more minute. If you don't open that safe, you're a dead man."

"Take your time, Ernie," Gorman urged. "A minute's a long time."

Pohlman's face was white and wet with sweat. He carefully turned the dial again, heard the tumblers click and slumped with relief. He dumped the contents of the money box on the floor. Palmer nodded to Bill Kuehnel and said, "Now, sir, I want you to get the bills from the wallets and put all the money into that paper bag."

When Kuehnel had completed his task, Gorman said to Palmer, "You've got all we can give you. Why don't you take off?"

Palmer ignored the suggestion and stared at the men for a minute. "Brother," he said to Gorman, "write out a sign saying 'Closed till 1 p.m.' and put it on the window of the front door." Palmer seemed to have a plan in mind.

Gorman penciled the words on a rectangle of cardboard. As

he taped the sign to the door window, he saw a man step onto the porch of the house across the street. He kept rubbing the sign, hoping to attract the man's attention. But Palmer grew aware of his excess motions and said, "Brother, you're having a hard time with that sign. Get away from there." Each time Palmer gave an order, he moved the rifle decisively.

Palmer then addressed the group: "Do any of you have a knife?" Nobody answered. To Kuehnel, he said, "Take a piece of glass, sir, and cut that telephone wire." Palmer seemed to enjoy using the word "sir" in giving orders.

After Kuehnel had cut the cord, Palmer asked, "Is there any rope around here?" Again nobody answered, although Gorman and his employees knew there was rope in the shed behind the building.

To Gorman, Palmer repeated, "Is there any rope?"

"On top of that elevator outside." Gorman pointed to the elevated sand-and-gravel bin and cement chute about forty feet away. A wood ladder rose from the ground to the top of the bin where two lengths of rope dangled.

Palmer spoke to Kuehnel. "You, sir, get up that ladder and bring down a rope." As Kuehnel started out, Palmer said, "Wait! It might not look right unless it was the owner." He nodded at Gorman. "Better if you did it, brother."

He ordered the seven other men to lie on their bellies, face to the floor and hands behind their backs. "Not a false move out of any of you," he warned, "or your boss'll get it." He posted himself at the door and told Gorman to climb the ladder and get the rope. "And if you try anything funny, there are going to be a lot of dead men in here."

Gorman climbed the ladder. As he began fooling with the rope, he stood close to the top edge of the sand bin. He wanted terribly to be free of Palmer. I could roll into the sand bin and

Palmer could never hit me, he thought. Then I'd yell for help. Maybe when the men heard me they could make a break for it. But, no, Palmer would start shooting. Gorman gathered up the rope and climbed down.

In the office, Palmer told Gorman to tie the men's hands behind their backs as they lay facedown on the floor. First in line was Kuehnel. As the railroad man felt the rope go around his wrists he resigned himself to death. "I figured this was my time," he later recalled. "I knew he was going to shoot us."

Palmer tested the knot and said, "Brother, you tie a loose knot. If I find another knot like that, I'm going to shoot the man through the head."

Gorman retied the knot. Then he bound Fitzgibbons' wrists. "As the seven of us lay there," Fitzgibbons said later, "I swear I felt the floor vibrate from our heartbeats." Gorman was feeling sick at the thought that he was tying up the men so that Palmer could shoot them while helpless. This was the killer's pattern, he knew.

After Gorman had tied the wrists of the next man, Darrell Smith, Palmer said, "Three down and four to go. When they're all tied up, I'll have to shoot them through the head." On the floor the silent men lay tense as boards, listening to the blood pound in their ears, waiting for the shots.

"I was never more scared in my life," Gorman later recalled, "but I knew I had to do something. If I lunged at Palmer, I'd probably get a bullet in the head. If I simply obeyed him, I'd still get the bullet in the head and so would seven other men."

Palmer sat alertly on his haunches, his rifle muzzle following Gorman's every move. Gorman, about seven feet away, knew that if he tied up the fourth man, he'd be a step farther away from the killer. He had to contrive a means of getting closer.

During his seventy-five minutes of captivity Gorman had noticed that whenever Palmer rose from his haunches he invariably pointed his rifle at the ceiling before bringing it to bear on his victims. If attacked, would Palmer stick to this habit, giving his assailant an added fraction of a second—or would he fire from his haunched position?

Gorman said, "Their legs are too jammed together for me to step between them."

"Then step on their legs, brother. They won't be hurting for long."

"I'll be able to do a better job if I can work from around their heads," Gorman said. This would put him a little closer to Palmer.

"You have my permission," Palmer said.

Then Gorman had a sudden idea, felt his guts twist in fear, and acted. He stepped between the second and third man and, without haste, pretended to stumble. He tottered, then, in a seeming effort to regain his balance, stepped over the second man, moving closer to Palmer. To make the action seem innocent he stepped *backward,* giving the killer a clear shot at his back. Again Gorman took a step backward, over the remaining man between him and Palmer.

The killer hesitated a moment, then—following habit—rose from his haunches, pointing the rifle toward the ceiling. In the split moment it took Palmer to bring the rifle down, Gorman was next to him and felt the gun barrel on his shoulder. He swung his left fist at the trigger guard, scraping the skin off his knuckles as he knocked the gun from Palmer's hands. Then, with all his power, he shot his right fist at Palmer's jaw. The killer went down, and Gorman fell on him. Palmer groped for the gun six inches away. Gorman jammed a knee on his wrist and hit him again, yelling, "Come on, boys!"

Galvanized into action, the four free men dived at Palmer. As they subdued him, contractor Ralph Russell came in the door. Hearing the scuffling and exclamations, he peered over the counter and said, "What's going on, a crap game this time of the morning?"

One of the men looked up and grunted, "Palmer!" Charlie Kroeschel ran to the nearest telephone. In three minutes the sheriff's car skidded to a halt in front of the office. Deputies handcuffed Palmer, now meek and whimpering a little, and hauled him away. It was all over.

Gorman and the seven men stood staring at one another. The thought of what might have happened was coursing through each of them like an electric shock. Gorman looked at his bloody hand. Then, in a dazed but businesslike tone he said, "Okay, boys, we've got concrete to haul."

That broke the spell. Almost in chorus, the four truck drivers demanded, "Who the hell is going to haul it?"

Gorman felt a flush of relief, and grinned. "This morning," he said, "I guess nobody is."

For his brave action Louis Gorman received the Silver Medal of the Carnegie Hero Fund Commission. Palmer is serving a 180-year prison term and will not be out—unless paroled—until 2020, when he will be 82.

James Gordon Palmer was released on parole in 1984 after serving twenty-five years.

THE SPY'S SON

by Bryan Denson

Nathan Nicholson strolled out of a Hilton hotel on Cyprus, map in hand, looking like any other American tourist eager to be charmed by the Mediterranean isle. But this was no sightseeing excursion. The young man from Eugene, Oregon, was so keyed up for his meeting with the Russian spy he knew as George that he'd arrived an hour early for their street-side rendezvous.

Just as George had instructed, Nathan clutched a backpack in his right hand and wore the khaki baseball cap the Russian had given him at their last meeting in Lima, Peru.

At precisely 7 p.m., Nathan caught a glimpse of the gray-haired spy walking up the sidewalk. He waited for George to speak.

"Can you show me the way to the federal post office?" George's English was excellent as always.

Nathan raised his map. He felt ridiculous reciting his end of their rehearsed dialogue. They had met face-to-face three times, and both knew why they were there. But he didn't want to disappoint George.

"It should be around here somewhere," he said. "Let me show you the way."

Soon, Nathan found himself lying across the backseat of a foreign sedan with two Russians yakking in their native tongue as they bumped along the old streets into an underground garage.

There George led him up a narrow stairwell into a room with thick walls. Nathan handed over a six-page handwritten document and collected $12,000 in U.S. hundred-dollar bills. The two men agreed to meet a year later in Bratislava, Slovakia.

Back at his hotel, Nathan paid his bill and headed for the airport. His plane touched down in Portland early on December 15, 2008, and he drove home to Eugene as snow threw a blanket over the shoulders of the Willamette Valley.

He reached his apartment at 3:30 a.m. and stashed the money in his nightstand. Then he collapsed in the loopy delirium known only to those who've flown halfway around the world in coach.

At 1:20 p.m., a loud pounding startled him awake. He stumbled out of bed to find two FBI agents at his door.

* * *

The vision of the agents at his doorstep transported Nathan back a dozen years to one of the most punishing days of his life—a chilly November Saturday in northern Virginia, 1996, when two unsmiling adults walked up to his home and knocked on the door. They produced search warrants declaring that Nathan's dad—Jim Nicholson, whose nickname in the CIA was Batman—had been arrested for espionage.

Jim, the CIA had learned, had spent the mid-1990s selling U.S. secrets to Russian spies from Singapore to Switzerland. The American agent with the Rolex watch, bespoke suits, and a .40-caliber Glock gave up classified files, including the identities of CIA trainees, some he had mentored himself. Jim was the highest-ranking CIA officer convicted of espionage, and his breaches forced the CIA to cancel sensitive operations and yank highly trained spies from the field.

Nathan, then 12, felt like he was losing the father he had just come to know. The CIA job had kept his dad away from home for weeks at a time. But things changed after his parents split up and Jim got primary custody of the three kids—Nathan, older brother Jeremi, and older sister Star. Jim finally began to balance his career and his role as father, Boy Scout adviser, soccer coach, and chauffeur.

But now he wasn't coming home. Three months after his arrest, Jim pleaded guilty to conspiracy to commit espionage in exchange for a lighter prison term. He was allowed to serve his time in Oregon, where his children had moved.

The former CIA man told a court official that he hoped, before he died, to offer his children a positive example.

* * *

Jim entered the prison in Sheridan in July 1997, a week before Nathan's 13th birthday. A few months later, he sat his children down to clear the air about his crime.

In a soft voice with his chin dropped nearly to his chest, he admitted he had indeed sold U.S. secrets to the Russians for money. Nathan recalls his words: "I just wanted to help you kids out."

The three kids hugged their dad and jokingly warned him not to do it again. In the years ahead, they would log hundreds of hours in the prison visiting room, sharing the ups and downs of their teens and 20s—car troubles, love interests, college loans.

But Jim's words on that weekend churned in Nathan's mind long afterward. He was convinced the government had set up his dad, forcing him to confess—even to his kids—that he was a turncoat. Nathan was determined not to believe a word of it.

* * *

Jim confided to an inmate in his prayer circle that he felt like a failure because of his children's financial miseries. By the middle of 2006, Jeremi was sweating college loans on the pay of an Air Force senior airman. Star faced car problems and a student loan debt of $50,000. Nathan was struggling to make payments on his rent, car, and credit card.

One day, as Nathan sat shoulder to shoulder with his dad in the prison visiting room, Jim said he had a plan.

He whispered to Nathan that his old friends in Moscow might give them financial assistance. The way Jim figured it, he had lost his freedom helping the Russian Federation; it seemed only fitting for the Russians to help his kids while he was away. Jim's plan was to slip messages to Nathan, who would carry them to a Russian consulate. "It's dangerous," he warned his son.

Nathan knew his dad's CIA days were animated by such intrigue, and he couldn't wait to prove his mettle. Jim described the days ahead as risky but not illegal—and Nathan believed him.

On October 13, 2006, at about 10 a.m., Nathan entered the Russian consulate in San Francisco and slid his dad's introductory note to a receptionist. She read it slowly, asked him to take a seat, and walked away.

An hour later, he met with a man with a mustache and a thick Russian accent, who clearly doubted he was the son of Russia's former CIA mole. Nevertheless, he said to come back in precisely two weeks.

On October 27, Nathan headed south again. When he walked into the Russian consulate, his contact with the mustache was a changed man. He hugged Nathan, asked about his family, and said to call him Mike.

The FBI would later identify Mike as Mikhail I. Gorbunov, a Russian diplomat assigned to San Francisco.

Gorbunov handed Nathan a brown paper bag stuffed with $5,000 and gave him the address of the Russian embassy in Mexico City, where he would meet a new handler in six weeks. Nathan couldn't believe his good luck; his dad's plan had actually come together. On the drive back to Eugene, Nathan's cell phone rang. It was Jim. He wanted to make sure his boy was rested enough for the long drive home. Nathan interjected that he had good news.

"I made a sale for $5K," he said.

Also, he said, he might be heading to Mexico.

Surreptitiously using napkins he picked up for snacks he bought for his dad, Nathan had found a way around prison rules that forbade the exchange of notes in the visiting room. On his trip to Mexico City in late 2006, he carried with him two paper-napkin notes from his dad.

His new host in Mexico City introduced himself as George and asked about his father's health and his family's debts. He let Nathan know the Russians were there to help.

Nathan handed George the two notes. Jim had asked for money for his family and let the Russians know he would assist them if he could.

George gave Nathan an assignment. He wanted him to get details from his dad about his 1996 arrest, including the identities of the FBI agents who interrogated him and the name of a CIA polygraph examiner. George also wanted to know when Jim first suspected he had fallen under surveillance and hoped to learn when Jim was turned down for a station chief job in Ethiopia.

Nathan scribbled in a pocket notebook as George shook out $10,000 in U.S. hundred-dollar bills, careful not to touch them. George ended their meeting by setting up another one, same place, the following July.

Nathan's faith in the old man was paying off. There was enough to fix Star's failing car, send some cash to his big brother, and pay his own debts—all in time for Christmas. "I felt like an undercover Santa Claus," he recalls.

*   *   *

Just before Christmas, Nathan updated his dad about his trip. The former spy told his son he'd performed better than some of the CIA trainees he'd once taught. Nathan, basking in the accolades, was beginning to feel like Robin to Jim's Batman. "You have been brave enough to step into this new unseen world that is sometimes dangerous but always fascinating," Jim later wrote to his son. "God leads us on our greatest adventures. Keep looking through your new eyes." But Jim was preaching to the converted. Nathan was thrilled to be working as his dad's spy kid.

In July 2007, Nathan flew back to Mexico City and handed George Jim's latest notes, which gave up the name of a government polygraph examiner and described the FBI agents who interrogated him. Nathan pocketed another $10,000.

Agents had been reading Jim's correspondence for years. Now they detected a suspicious spike in his letters to Nathan and got permission from the Foreign Intelligence Surveillance Court in Washington, D.C., to eavesdrop on the young spy.

In October 2007, the FBI searched Nathan's apartment in Eugene and copied the hard drives of his computers and stacks of photos and papers. On December 10, they were still testing a GPS monitor they'd planted on his Chevy Cavalier when it showed the car parked at the Portland airport. They learned Nathan had boarded a plane for Lima and would be returning through Houston.

After the plane landed, Jared Garth, the supervising agent in the Nicholson investigation, asked a U.S. Customs and Border Protection officer to cull Nathan from the herd of travelers. As Garth looked on, the customs official pawed through Nathan's backpack, pulling out a camera, thousands of dollars, and more important, a notebook. Nathan silently freaked out as he watched his notebook disappear into an adjacent office. Inside the book's 160 pages, he had jotted down the Russians' questions and other notes sure to raise suspicion, including his code name, Dick, and the address of the Russian consulate in Lima. In the office, Garth copied down everything in the notebook. An hour later, Nathan was told he was free to go. He bolted for his gate like a kid sprinting from the cops.

Nathan began to worry. His meetings with the Russians seemed wrong, probably even illegal, but he wanted to believe that his dad wouldn't steer him into a crime. So he pressed ahead, confirming his next rendezvous with George in Cyprus—his fourth meeting with the Russian spy in the past two years.

*   *   *

Now, on December 15, 2008, Nathan lurched out of bed heavy-legged with jet lag. He opened his door to Jared Garth and his partner, Special Agent John Cooney, who introduced themselves as FBI agents and said they were looking for help with an investigation.

The agents got Nathan talking about himself, then got around to asking him about his trips abroad.

Nathan, who had served three years in the Army, obliged them with a spectacular run of lies: He had saved his Veterans Affairs checks to travel on three continents. Met up with Army pals. Checked out local architecture. Even scouted places to propose marriage to his girlfriend.

Cooney, a certified polygraph operator, let Nathan go on for about two hours before reminding him that it's against the law to lie to a federal agent and that the FBI knew more about his travels than he was telling. Cooney leaned on golf lexicon, telling Nathan he had whiffed a few times and would now get a one-time-only "mulligan," or do-over.

Nathan had feared this day for months. His worries, he says, had given him ulcers and caused spells of disorientation.

He took the mulligan.

He felt like a rat implicating his dad in their plot but held a glimmer of hope that the old man had been right: Smuggling his notes to the Russians and accepting their money wasn't illegal.

Nathan signed a confession as an FBI team searched his apartment. He asked if the agents were going to arrest him.

Not tonight, Garth said.

* * *

That same day, FBI agents Scott Jensen and Tony Buckmeier sat down with Jim Nicholson at the federal prison in Sheridan. Jensen, known for a wit drier than cheatgrass, began by laying a postcard on the table with big yellow letters: "Greetings from Cyprus." He told his suspect that the FBI knew all about Nathan's travels.

The former CIA man told the agents that if they were trying to implicate him and his son in a crime, he wanted a lawyer. So the agents ended the interview.

Jim was sent to a 23-hour-a-day solitary unit known as the hole. He was forbidden to communicate in any way with Nathan. It would be 764 days until he again laid eyes on his son.

* * *

After the FBI cleared out, Nathan checked his cell phone. There were messages from his cousins, mom, brother, and sister—all interviewed by the FBI and worried sick about him. Nathan called Star. "What's up with the FBI?" she asked. It's a long story, Nathan said. He explained that he'd been transporting information and getting paid for it.

Star wanted to know who got the information.

"Well," Nathan said, dreading the words to follow, "it was for the Russians."

"Dude!"

Nathan told Star not to worry, he hadn't done anything illegal. He also told her that the thousands of dollars she and Jeremi had gotten over the past couple of years hadn't come from their grandparents' suddenly booming craft sales, as she had been told.

"That was you?" she asked.

"Yeah."

"Dude, you're not supposed to do that," Star said. Not that she didn't appreciate the money, she told her younger brother. "But you know, seriously, it sounds kind of like what Daddy did."

For six weeks after his confession to the FBI, Nathan Nicholson slept on the floor, punishing himself for the trouble he had caused.

"I envisioned my dad in a concrete cell and being treated very harshly," Nathan recalls. "I felt equally responsible for what had happened, and I didn't feel that it would be fair if I wasn't disciplined."

On January 28, 2009, discipline came knocking.

Nathan was catnapping on the floor of his Eugene apartment on that gusty, gray Wednesday when two FBI agents rapped on his door. Nathan recognized Jared Garth, one of the agents who had initially interviewed him. He knew why they were there.

Garth handcuffed Nathan and loaded him into the back of his Ford Crown Victoria for the two-hour drive to the Justice Center jail in downtown Portland. He reminded Nathan that it was his dad who had sold out his country to the Russians and later orchestrated their plot to pass new messages to Moscow. It was Jim, said Garth, who had used manipulative powers— sharpened in the CIA—on his own son. It was time, he said, to be his own man.

Nathan wept.

He had spent more than half his life visiting his father behind bars. Soon it was he who fell into the familiar rhythms of confinement, his hours clocked by the movement of food carts, the brightening and dimming of fluorescent lights, and the ceaseless murmur of men's voices.

Around the same time, after a little more than a month in the hole, Jim asked to see Jensen. He said he hoped to protect his son from any criminal charges.

The prosecutors weren't interested. They indicted father and son on charges of money laundering, acting as agents of a foreign government, and conspiracy. The money-laundering charge alone carried up to 20 years in prison.

After more than two months in jail, Nathan was sprung to await trial. He concluded that his best hope of staying out of prison was pleading guilty and cooperating with the government. That fall, Nathan met with prosecutors and FBI agents and gave up more details of his two years on the road. With each revelation, he felt as if he were plunging a knife into his father's back.

On one hand, federal agents were telling him that Jim had manipulated him; on the other hand, he adored his dad, whose plot seemed designed to help his family. Forbidden to communicate with Jim, Nathan prepared himself for the witness box.

"I had to essentially crucify him," he recalls.

* * *

Last fall, as he met with a prosecutor, Nathan started to learn how deeply he had trespassed in the global spy game.

George was the nom de guerre of Vasiliy V. Fedotov, a retired KGB general who had once headed Moscow's efforts to penetrate the U.S. intelligence apparatus. Fedotov posed such a threat to national security during a Cold War posting in Washington, D.C., that the United States kicked him out of the country.

Russia's foreign intelligence service, the SVR, had hired Fedotov to find out whether someone inside its own intelligence ranks had informed the U.S. government, back in the mid-1990s, about a traitor inside the CIA who was selling secrets to Russia. That traitor was Jim Nicholson.

* * *

As Nathan prepped for trial, Jim and his lawyer, Samuel C. Kauffman, staked out a bold defense strategy. In pretrial court papers, he conceded his client sought financial help from Russia but argued it wasn't illegal, even for someone convicted of spying for Russia, to ask Moscow for money.

Privately, though, Jim had serious misgivings about putting Nathan through a courtroom showdown, Kauffman says. "Ultimately, he couldn't move forward."

Last November, Jim decided to plead guilty in exchange for eight additional years in prison. With time off for good behavior, he would get out in his early 70s. Nathan was overjoyed that he might one day see his dad beyond prison walls.

On the morning of December 7, Nathan stood nervously before U.S. District Judge Anna J. Brown for sentencing. The judge leafed through papers, noting that Nathan had met all his obligations to the government. She agreed with lawyers on both sides of the case that the 72 days he had spent in jail were enough.

"A prison sentence," she said, "isn't necessary."

Brown sentenced him to five years' supervised probation and 100 hours of community service.

*   *   *

At Jim's sentencing a month later, Judge Brown offered him a chance to say a few words. "Your Honor, in my life I have been through several coups, a revolution, and a war," he said. "I have been marked for assassination by a foreign terrorist organization, been hunted by armed gunmen in East Asia, and imprisoned in this country. I have gone through a heart-wrenching divorce and custody battle.

"But the worst day of my life was the day I learned that my young son had been arrested and charged with acts for which I am responsible."

Jim said he watched, as if in amber, as his kids struggled to make ends meet. He had reached out to the one source he could think of for help: Russia.

"And insofar as their efforts were truly to help my children, I regret the embarrassment that this has caused them as well."

Jim asked his children to forgive him and described Nathan's efforts as selfless.

"I love him dearly," he said. "I could not be more proud of him. He has never let me down, and he has never failed his family. Any failure has been mine alone."

Nathan wept quietly as Brown glared at his dad.

"He's made an eloquent statement here today to his family, to his children," she said. "Notably absent from his remarks, however, was any suggestion of remorse for committing criminal conduct against the United States and its interests. What he calls previous assistance to the Russian Federation was criminal espionage."

Jared Garth, in the courtroom for the sentencing was astounded by Jim's apology to the Russians rather than the United States. Later, it dawned on him: "Why would he apologize to the United States? He was loyal to the Russian Federation."

Jim is now being held at a medium-security prison in Terre Haute, Indiana. He and his son can no longer talk or write to each other without approval of Nathan's probation officer.

On a recent afternoon in Corvallis, where he studies computer science at Oregon State University, Nathan pondered a question he would pose to his dad if they could sit down together:

Had Jim, in trying to help his kids, considered the risks?

"I feel like we ended up hurting the family more," Nathan admits.

And his country—had Nathan betrayed it?

"Absolutely," he says.

His father's projected release date is June 27, 2024, about a month shy of Nathan's 40th birthday. By then, Jim's boy hopes to have a wife and three kids of his own.

He will tell them his dad is a loving man who made mistakes and suffered terribly for them.

"He was my hero," Nathan says unwaveringly. "Still is."

Jim Nicholson is now being held at a maximum-security prison in Florence, Colorado. His projected release date is still June 27, 2024. Nathan graduated from Oregon State University with a degree in computer science and now works as a web designer. He is no longer on probation.

THE DRIVE OF HIS LIFE

by Paul Kix
from *GQ*

"**T**ake us to Walmart," said the man who settled into the passenger seat. The driver, Long Ma, 71, recognized from his voice that he was the one who'd called for the cab, telling Ma that he and his friends needed a ride home from a restaurant. His name was Bac Duong. He spoke to Ma in Vietnamese—their shared native language—and wore a salt-and-pepper goatee on his thin and weary face. It was 9:30 on a chilly Friday night in Santa Ana, California. Now they want to go shopping? Ma thought. What happened to going home? Ma, a small man with short gray hair and a gray mustache, had been asleep when Duong called and hadn't bothered changing out of his pajamas.

In the rearview mirror, Ma could see Duong's friends, quiet in the back seat: Jonathan Tieu, a pimply 20-year-old, and Hossein Nayeri, an athletic Persian with an air of indifference.

Walmart didn't have what the men needed, so they told Ma to drive them to a Target 45 minutes away. Ma had no way of knowing that they were desperate for phones, for clothes, and for some semblance of a plan. They finally emerged from Target. "My mom's place is right around here," Duong lied. "Take us there, please."

The streets were dark and quiet, and after a few minutes,

Duong motioned to a mangy strip mall. "Pull in here," he said. As Ma parked his Honda Civic, Tieu handed Duong a pistol, which Duong pointed at Ma. Ma's mind raced as Nayeri shouted, "Boom, boom, old man!"

The men placed Ma in the back seat, where Tieu now trained the gun on his stomach. Nayeri jumped behind the wheel and set out for a nearby motel.

By the time they arrived, Ma was convinced he was going to die—he just didn't know how or when. Inside a cramped room, he watched as Nayeri, who he suspected was the group's ringleader, splayed out on one of the two beds. Ma was ordered to double up with Duong on the other as Tieu slept on the floor near the door, the gun under his pillow. For Ma, there was no escape and, with all the dread he felt, no easy way to fall asleep.

In the morning, Duong turned on the TV. A report about a prison escape was on the news. "Hey," Duong shouted, "that's us!" Mug shots filled the screen. A massive manhunt, Ma now learned, was under way for his three roommates.

*　*　*

The jailbreak had occurred a day earlier, on January 22, 2016. It began after Duong, sprawled on a bunk in the open-floor dormitory of the Orange County Jail's Module F, watched a guard finish his 5 a.m. head count.

Duong then gathered the tools that he'd been hoarding and shuffled to the rear of the housing block, where Nayeri and Tieu waited for him. There, hidden behind a bunk bed, the three used their tools to work loose a metal grate. They bellied through the hole and, surrounded by pipes and wiring, inched along a metal walkway until it dead-ended against a wall. Using the pipes, they shinnied skyward into a ventilation shaft that led to a trapdoor, which they shoved open.

Now on the roof, they fastened a makeshift rope that they'd fashioned from bedsheets and rappelled down four stories to the ground. No alarms sounded; no lights swept the exterior. They'd done it. They were out.

The fugitives allegedly first visited friends, who gave them money. By 9 p.m., the escapees were still in Santa Ana and needed to get away. Duong dialed a cab service that advertised in the local Vietnamese newspaper. Long Ma answered the call.

As the men in the motel hooted and marveled at their images on the TV, Ma was introduced to his captors by their televised rap sheets. Tieu had allegedly taken part in a drive-by shooting that left one college-age kid dead; Duong had allegedly shot a man in the chest after an argument. And Nayeri, well, Nayeri was plenty notorious.

Four years earlier, acting on a hunch that the owner of a marijuana dispensary had buried $1 million in the Mojave Desert, Nayeri had allegedly snatched the guy and his roommate and driven them to the spot where the loot was thought to be hidden. There, Nayeri and his crew were said to have shocked the man with a Taser, burned him with a butane torch, and poured bleach on his wounds, among other abuses, all in a failed attempt to locate the cash. After the man assured Nayeri there was no buried money, he was left out there to die. (His roommate found help and saved his life.)

Spooked, perhaps, by the prospect that Ma's disappearance had been noticed, the escapees decided they needed a second vehicle. The next morning, they found a van for sale on Craigslist. Duong took the vehicle for a test spin and then simply drove away. He met up with the others again later, and the fugitives visited a hair salon and altered their appearances, none more than Duong, who shaved his goatee and dyed his hair black.

When they left the salon, Nayeri and Tieu took the van. Duong and Ma got into the Civic, and there, alone in the car, Duong became relaxed and even chatty, asking about the cabbie's life in their native Vietnamese. At one point, he even called Ma "Uncle," a term of endearment that implied respect for the old man. But Ma was leery. For all he knew, Duong was playing an angle. As always in the States, Ma found his fellow Vietnamese the hardest people to read.

When Ma had landed in California in 1992, with a wife and four kids, he'd struggled. A former lieutenant colonel in the South Vietnamese Army during the Vietnam War, he still had the physical and emotional scars from seven punishing years spent in a Communist forced-labor camp. The war and his time in the camp had placed him nearly two decades behind the first wave of emigrants who'd left Vietnam for the United States. For years he took menial jobs, and he would later say that his siblings—who had arrived earlier and become dentists and pharmacists and white-collar success stories—made him feel ashamed of the life he had made.

Money had always been tight, which exacerbated the arguments between Ma and his wife. He knew she was losing respect for him and that everyone in the family had noticed it. Rather than suffer the indignity, Ma moved one day, without explanation, from their home in San Diego. He found a little room in a boardinghouse near Santa Ana, 90 minutes north, and began a solitary existence as a taxi driver—a choice that seemed to have led to his current predicament.

* * *

Duong steered the Civic toward a new motel, the Flamingo Inn, where they would meet Nayeri and Tieu. Deep into the night, the fugitives laughed and drank and smoked cigarettes, while on television the news anchors said that the reward for information leading to their arrest had increased from $20,000 to $50,000.

Sunday dawned, and Nayeri seemed more distant than usual. Ma's captors drank and talked in urgent tones. Nayeri soon began yelling at Duong. The room became loud and tense and small. Ma, with his limited English, sensed that the argument concerned him. He'd begun to consider what the men must have realized themselves: If they killed him now, they could make a cleaner escape. Ma watched as Nayeri pointed in his direction and again shouted, "Boom, boom, old man!"

The escapees decided they needed to move north, and on Tuesday morning—day four of Ma's captivity—they drove 350 stressful miles to a motel in San Jose. The journey exhausted Ma, and that night he snored so loudly that he woke Duong, who was lying beside him. But Duong didn't elbow him awake. Instead, he slowly climbed out of bed, careful not to stir Ma, and curled up on the floor, so Uncle might rest more peacefully.

The next day, Nayeri announced that he and Tieu needed to take Ma out for a while in the van. By the time they parked near the ocean in Santa Cruz, Ma had figured he'd been driven to the beach to be executed. His stroll with Nayeri and Tieu began aimlessly—and because of that, it felt even more malevolent to Ma. Nayeri had them pose for pictures. With the ocean, the beach, and the pier as their backdrop, Nayeri acted as if they were friends. What is he doing? Ma thought. And then . . . nothing. The three got in the van and drove back to the motel.

After watching another news report on themselves, Nayeri and Duong started shouting at each other. Suddenly, Nayeri glanced at Ma and ran his index finger across his throat. In an instant, days of anger and anxiety broke, and Nayeri and

Duong fell into a rolling heap. Nayeri ended up on top and landed a series of clean shots to Duong's nose and jaw, one after another. Satisfied, Nayeri pulled himself out of his rage. Each man gasped for air.

Ma was terrified. But Nayeri did not grab the gun and shoot the cabdriver. He did not haul the old man outside and, in the shadows of the motel, slit his throat. Nayeri simply retreated to a corner. For another night, the four watched one another and, as they went to bed, stewed in the frustration that filled the room.

The news reports were no better the next morning—their seventh day on the run. Law enforcement shared photos of the stolen van the men were driving. This rattled Nayeri and Tieu, who announced to Duong that they were leaving to have the van's windows tinted and its license plates changed.

When the door closed behind them, Duong turned quickly to Ma. "Uncle, we have to go," he said in Vietnamese.

* * *

The two men drove south in Ma's Civic, with Duong behind the wheel. When Duong said to him, "Don't be afraid; you're not in danger anymore," Ma snickered to himself. We'll see, he thought. He had understood enough of the news to piece together Duong's criminal past: a 1995 burglary conviction in San Diego, four years after he became a U.S. resident; twice pleading guilty to selling cocaine; stints in state prison; and then, in November 2015, the alleged attempted murder of a Santa Ana man after an argument.

And yet, in spite of Duong's past, there had been, this whole week, another composite on view: that of a flawed but compassionate man. Ma had caught flashes of details but not the full picture of Duong's conflicted life. He didn't realize how chronic drug dependency and what Duong's friends saw as

mental disorders had pushed Duong down a criminal path—
and he didn't yet know that Duong was also the father of two
boys, Peter and Benny.

Duong, his eyes filling with tears, told Ma that he hated how
his crimes had placed him outside society. That was the most
painful thing—not being accepted. His father wouldn't speak to
him, and his mother said she was ashamed. A few years earlier,
out of prison after serving a drug sentence, Duong had asked
his friend Theresa Nguyen and her husband to go with him to
his mother's home—"Because I want her to know that I have
normal friends, too," he told Nguyen. He could never atone in
his family's eyes. Nguyen began to get it, why Duong had been
calling her "Sister." Why he'd phoned her the day her daughter
graduated from college, another immigrant success story: "I'm
proud of you, Sister." She was as close to family as he had.

Ma listened, reticent but knowing that sometimes people
need to be heard even more than consoled.

Duong told Ma that Nayeri's plan had been to kill the driver
on the beach. But for whatever reason, Nayeri hadn't gone
through with it. The brutal fight the night before had been
over Ma too. Duong couldn't abide seeing the cabdriver murdered for Duong's mistakes.

Ma said at last, "You should turn yourself in."

Duong didn't balk at the suggestion. He was grateful for the
way Ma hadn't judged him. He didn't want to call Ma "Uncle"
anymore, he said. Given the circumstances of the past week,
Duong said he wanted to call Ma "Father."

The suggestion moved Ma, who understood the cultural ob-
ligation that came with the moniker: To call Duong "Son." To
trust him, to love him, even. This scared Ma. Life had taught
him to be cautious around love. And yet when he looked at the
damaged man next to him, his face bruised from the fight with

Nayeri, his psyche scarred, he saw the good that the rest of the world failed to see. It warmed him.

"Yes," Ma said. "You can call me 'Father,' and I will call you 'Son.'"

After hours on the road, they pulled up to an auto-repair shop in Santa Ana. As instructed, Ma slunk inside the garage while Duong sat in the car. In a moment, the old man returned with a woman, who put her head inside the vehicle. Duong started to cry. "Sister," he said to Nguyen, "I'm tired."

*   *   *

The day after Duong turned himself in, Tieu and Nayeri were captured in San Francisco after police were alerted to their van parked on a city street. Ma returned to his boardinghouse. No one had even reported him missing.

Though Duong is back in jail now, Ma has stayed in touch. And while money is scarce for the cabdriver, he has put cash in Duong's jail account. Ma has even visited the man who kidnapped him. The last time he went, Ma watched through a glass partition as Duong, in an orange jumpsuit, bowed when they met. "Daddy Long!" Duong said, greeting his friend.

Throughout their half-hour visit, the two men wept softly and spoke in their native language of the bond they had nurtured since their week on the run. They both felt so grateful, so surprised by the possibility of friendship. Perhaps Ma especially. Whatever he had expected to experience on that dark, cold night when he left his house in his pajamas, it wasn't this. Wherever he'd figured that trip might lead, it wasn't here.

As Ma grinned through the glass of the visitors' room wall, he realized that Duong had saved his life, even redeemed his soul.

"My son," Ma said to Duong, "as long as you are still here, I will rescue you like you rescued me."

THE INTRUDER

by Andrea Cooper

About 6:30 on a sunny autumn morning, a man high on methamphetamine wandered aimlessly through a San Jose residential neighborhood, prowling through yards, testing back doors. When one clicked open, nineteen-year-old Marcus Allen Paden slipped inside the home of Suzanne and Tom Marotti.

* * *

Noises. Sinking down through levels of consciousness. Strange sounds that gradually became voices fading in and out. Suzanne Marotti was sleeping in one of her kids' bedrooms to get away from her husband Tom's snoring. But this wasn't snoring. Maybe the kids had turned on the TV. The voices became louder. Swearing. Screaming.

* * *

All Suzanne Marotti ever wanted was to be a princess. In her early 20s, she was a carefree girl who would hop into a friend's car at midnight and head off to Los Angeles just for fun. A jewelry saleswoman, Suzanne earned a good salary and liked to spend it.

Then Tom Marotti strolled into the store to buy a ring. Suzanne was immediately attracted to his body-builder physique and confident manner. He asked her out. She told him she didn't date customers. But he kept asking. And a fiery romance followed.

Tom, a construction foreman, was used to women who were seen and not heard. Suzanne said he could forget that attitude. "Nobody is going to tell me what to do."

And so they married.

Tom rebuilt a modest house into a 3000-square-foot home. He took Suzanne out dancing and on vacations to Las Vegas. If his princess wanted new furniture or a car, she got them.

Then Suzanne learned she was pregnant. And life began to change. In the seventh month she felt a lump in her neck. Doctors diagnosed Hodgkin's lymphoma. Two months after Tommy was born, Suzanne had surgery to remove a cancerous spleen. Nine months of chemotherapy followed, and eventually doctors proclaimed that she was in remission.

During this time Tom also faced a frightening situation. Walking upstairs, he lost his balance and fell—it was the first sign of multiple sclerosis.

Struggling but determined, Tom continued to work at his construction business and Suzanne became pregnant again. But just days after Matthew was born, Tom said his partners asked him to leave the company because he wasn't pulling his weight.

So slowly, the princess became the breadwinner—eventually opening her own jewelry store the year her third son, Daniel, was born. Her family and her love for Tom were growing—but so were their difficulties. As Tom gradually lost control of his limbs, Suzanne found a caregiver, Todd Leach, who moved in to help Tom.

* * *

Suzanne ran toward the screaming in the master bedroom. She stopped in shock at the doorway. An intruder was holding a knife to Tom's throat.

"Who the hell are you?" Suzanne yelled in disbelief. The stranger didn't respond. "Don't hurt him!" she pleaded. "He can't even walk. Look, there's a wheelchair."

The moment he glanced to the side, Suzanne charged. She jumped on the bed and grabbed his wrist. "Who are you? What do you want?" she cried.

"You better back off!" the man said.

Though he was unable to move, it was not in Tom's nature to back down. He tried to draw attention away from Suzanne, growling, "Go ahead. Do it, man. Come on. Bring it on!" That's the way he would have reacted before the MS, and he wasn't afraid now.

The commotion had also awakened Tommy, nine, who appeared at the bedroom door. Seeing the nightmarish scene inside, he began crying, "Please don't hurt my dad!"

"Go get Todd!" Suzanne yelled to her son.

*   *   *

In a downstairs bedroom, Todd Leach had also heard noises. At first he thought it was the TV or the Marottis having an argument. But there was an unfamiliar voice—and then a loud thud. Todd got up from bed to check it out and hurried to the master bedroom.

One look through the double doors and he froze. Tom was on the floor. A stranger was on the bed threatening Suzanne with a knife. He was tall, wiry, and had a wild look in his eyes.

"Todd, get him!" Suzanne cried.

Paden panicked and shot off the bed, knocking past Todd into the hallway, where Tommy was. The boy ran to his brother's bedroom and dived under the bed. Paden chased him and swiped his knife in a wide arc underneath, just missing the child.

Left alone in the bedroom, Tom felt his fear mounting—not for himself, but for his family for whom he could do nothing.

In the other bedroom, Paden saw two-year-old Daniel lying in bed. He grabbed the toddler by his arms, and began to shake him just as Suzanne and Todd burst into the room. Suzanne managed to throw herself between Paden and her son. "Get him out of here!" she yelled to Todd.

But as chance would have it, that was the very moment that four-year-old Matthew showed up, sleepy-eyed, from the hallway. Paden bolted past Suzanne, snatched Matthew and darted into the adjoining bathroom.

Paden jumped onto the toilet, perhaps thinking he could get out a small window above. He had one arm hooked around Matthew's throat—the little boy dangled in midair, his face contorted with fear. Suzanne and Todd came to an abrupt halt in the doorway.

"Back off, bitch! I'm going to kill him," Paden said to Suzanne. "You better get away."

"You hurt him, I swear I will kill you myself," she said.

Until that moment Suzanne had had no time to think—just react. It was all bizarre, unreal, but now for the first time she realized she was facing a madman who could kill her son, kill them all. *What should she do?* Negotiate with this guy? Matthew's his hostage. I'm not going to let anything happen to him. I'm not going to just stand by.

Once more she charged Paden—the force throwing the three of them to the floor.

Matthew wiggled free of his captor's grasp and ran to Todd. On her knees Suzanne struggled to escape. Paden pulled her back by the hair and brought the knife to her throat.

Todd tried to calm him. "It's okay. You don't have to do this," he said, holding out open hands, speaking soothingly. But as he stepped forward, the attacker grew more agitated. He pressed the knife to Suzanne's neck.

"I'm going to kill you. Don't move."

"Get the kids away!" Suzanne screamed. "Get the kids out!"

And, as if in a dream, she watched Todd back away with Matthew and slowly close the bathroom door.

*　*　*

Todd grabbed his cordless phone in the living room to call 911—and got a recorded message. Unwilling to wait any longer, he rushed the crying children out the front door, instructing them to run to a neighbor's house. Then he turned back inside. Passing the bathroom, he yelled to Suzanne that the children were safe and dashed to the phone to call 911 again. Finally there was an answer.

*　*　*

Sgt. Robert St. Amour was in early that morning. A member of the San Jose Police Department's Violent Crime Enforcement Team, he was preparing to issue an arrest warrant in another case when the emergency call came in.

Moments later he had cars rolling—lights flashing, sirens at full wail—to the Marottis' house. St. Amour listened to the details on the police band: *Assailant has broken into the home. Unknown male with a female hostage. Has a knife to her throat. Woman is fighting him off.*

St. Amour had been a police officer for 23 years. He knew the odds. Would the woman be alive when he got there?

*　*　*

"I'm cool, man. I won't fight you anymore," Suzanne told her captor. "Just don't hurt me." She had turned instinctively to a strategy she used selling jewelry. Be friendly. Keep talking.

"I am going to hurt you," Paden told her. "You better shut up."

"What do you want?"

"They're after me." He moved to a corner, dragging her by the hair.

Suzanne's mouth was dry. She had to keep him talking. "Do you smoke? I could really use a smoke."

"What, pot?"

"No, man, no pot. Cigarettes." She tried for a light tone. "What do you want? What are you doing here?"

"They're after me. They're going to kill me. I'm sorry, but I'll have to kill you too." Paden's eyes darted up and down, looking at the bathroom window. Again he pulled Suzanne across the floor by the hair.

"You're hurting me!" she screamed, and tried to hit him. Paden banged her head against the bathroom counter.

As Suzanne whimpered in agony, Paden's mood changed.

"I'm just a girl," she told him. "Don't you have any sisters?" She could see a small glimmer of life in his face.

"Yeah, I have a sister."

"You wouldn't want anybody to hurt her, would you?" She tried another tack. "You came to the wrong house. My name is Suzanne. We're the Marottis. What's your name?"

"It doesn't matter," he replied. "I'm already dead because I told. Now I'm taking you with me."

*   *   *

After calling 911, Todd ran to the bathroom and eased the door open. That agitated the intruder. Suzanne begged him to stay out. So he backed away and went to Tom. He picked him up and lifted him gently onto the bed.

"Do something!" Tom pleaded. "Bust the door down."

Todd was in a quandary. What could he do? He decided it was best to check outside to see if the cops were coming.

"Drop to your knees!" came a shouted command. Three policemen, two in front, one in back, had arrived and were covering the house. Todd fell to the ground, his hands in the air.

* * *

Again Suzanne tried to break free. As she struggled, the knife cut her finger. Blood flowed from the wound. "You cut me!" she said angrily, trying to gain the upper hand. "Get me a towel."

Paden flung back Suzanne's hair to see if he had cut her neck. Still clenching her hair close to her scalp, he gave her a towel. She tried to wrap her hand, but now Paden snatched it away—and forced her to the floor. Then he crawled on top of her.

This is it, Suzanne thought.

But he didn't try to rape her. He just rolled over her to the other side, and repositioned the knife from her neck to her heart, to her stomach, and back again in crazed fashion.

Suzanne was exhausted. She didn't know how to react. She needed a plan. But what? In the room down the hall, she could hear Tom screaming, "Suzanne! Suzanne!"

"I'm okay," she yelled back, though she was far from okay.

"Help! Somebody help my wife," Tom cried.

* * *

Paden was becoming ever more erratic. He pulled the top off the toilet tank and tried to barricade the window, but ended up smashing it. Glass fragments showered the floor. Suzanne was lying in them.

"I can hide you," she said, suddenly remembering that he had claimed someone was after him. "I've got an attic. There's stairs. I'll shut you in. They'll never find you."

At first he was silent. "What do you mean, you've got an attic?"

Suzanne told him she would hide him in the rafters where no one would look for him. She kept stalling for time.

As she was spinning out her tale, she heard footsteps in the hall. Paden heard them too. He jumped into the bathtub. Clenching her hair, he tried to drag Suzanne in with him. But she screamed with everything left in her.

*   *   *

The door burst open and Sergeant St. Amour and two officers crashed in. Stunned, Paden dropped his knife. But as the officers pulled him from the bathtub, he began to fight. St. Amour and the other cops wrestled him to the floor and bound his legs together.

During the scuffle, Suzanne crawled to safety. She was bloody, but alive. Her husband was alive. Her children were alive. She had fought with everything she had. And at last it was over.

*   *   *

Marcus Allen Paden spent several months undergoing treatment in a state psychiatric hospital. He then pleaded guilty to 12 felonies, including four charges of assault with a deadly weapon, four charges of felony false imprisonment and four charges of criminal threats. He also pleaded guilty to the misdemeanor of being under the influence of methamphetamine, which may explain in part his aberrant behavior on the day of the break-in.

For her instinctive response, quick action and courage, Suzanne Marotti received awards and accolades from the California State Senate and the San Jose Police Department. But the sweetest praise came from her husband, Tom. Knowing how the woman he loved had grown through illness and incredible testing, he said: "Seeing how she reacted to hardship made me love her even more. If there's anyone tougher than me, she is."

I HUNTED DOWN THE WOMAN WHO STOLE MY LIFE

by Anita Bartholomew

Karen Lodrick ordered a latte at Starbucks while waiting nervously for the bank on San Francisco's Market Street to open. She had been anxious and distracted of late but couldn't help noticing the scruffy-looking pair standing next to her: a tall man wearing a navy baseball jacket and a large woman in jeans and Gucci glasses, carrying a brown suede coat and a Prada purse. The woman looked vaguely familiar.

* * *

That coat. A cold tingle of fear ran through Karen as she took it all in. The distinctive faux-fur trim along its edges looked as unkempt as the woman who held it. And then—bingo—she knew. Karen's ID had been stolen five months before. Her bank account had been emptied, and her life sent reeling out of control. The coat she was looking at was the same one she'd seen in the bank surveillance tape, worn by the woman who'd stolen Karen's ID.

Karen followed the pair onto the patio and watched as they settled at a round table under a burgundy window awning. She called 911, asked that a police officer meet her, then settled at the next table, watching and waiting on this morning in April 2007.

Just the day before, Karen's bank had called after closing hours to tell her that she'd left her driver's license at a branch on Market and Church streets. But Karen had never been to that branch. And her real driver's license was still in her wallet.

The con artist must have come back to retrieve the phony license.

A cell call from her friend Ed Fuentes interrupted her thoughts. She walked toward the hedges that bordered the Starbucks patio, out of earshot of the pair, and told him her suspicions.

The large woman and her companion stole glances at Karen, looking increasingly nervous. Then they got up from the table and separated. The man turned south. The woman headed north.

"Ed, I've got to go," she told her friend. "I've got to follow her."

"Don't do anything crazy, Karen," said Fuentes. "She could have a gun."

"I've got to do it." She feared that if she didn't act, the identity thief would disappear, along with any hope of ending her bad dream. The chase was on.

For five months, the thief had dipped into Karen's accounts like they were her own private piggy bank. She scammed thousands of dollars more, using credit cards she opened in Karen's name. The banks were unable to stop her. The police could do nothing. Creditors demanded payment for the thief's transactions. Karen closed her accounts, only to have the criminal crack open the new ones she'd opened and drain those too.

The woman turned a corner. Karen's phone rang. The caller ID said "unknown caller." Karen looked up the street and saw that the woman had her cell phone out. Could she be checking to see if the real Karen Lodrick was on her tail? And where were the police?

As Karen approached a recycling center at the corner of Buchanan Street, a man stood looking quizzically at her, then at the woman she was following.

"Do you know her?" she asked.

"No. Do you?"

Karen told him she thought the woman had stolen her identity. "You're not the first person to say that about her," he said, arousing her suspicion about him as well. Was he an accomplice? Karen again called 911 as the woman took off up the hill, looking over her shoulder at Karen every few seconds.

"I need somebody to come to Buchanan and Market," Karen told the 911 operator who answered. "She is running. I need the police."

"What's the problem, ma'am?"

"This woman has been taking my identity. For the last five months. It's been a living hell."

* * *

There was an odd voice mail from Karen's bank waiting when she returned home to San Francisco in November 2006 from a family reunion in Michigan. Karen called back, and the service rep asked if she'd made any large withdrawals and mentioned one in the amount of $600. Karen assumed it was a bank error and asked the rep to verify the debit card number.

"That's not my card," she said.

The bank representative insisted—mistakenly, as Karen later learned—that someone had called from Karen's phone to order the new debit card. After much back-and-forth, Karen convinced the rep that it wasn't hers, and he canceled it. What he failed to mention was that a second new debit card had been issued on her account. And it was still open.

Concerned after the bank rep told her the order came from her home phone, Karen asked her neighbors if they'd heard about any break-ins. They hadn't. But several people in her building mentioned that they'd seen mailboxes hanging open. A thief had apparently broken into the mail and stolen at least four envelopes: two with debit cards and two that provided the debit card PINs.

As far as Karen knew, the thief had stolen $600. Bad enough, but not life-altering. It wasn't until she got to the bank, and a representative turned the computer screen around for her to see, that she understood what had occurred. Screen after screen showed dozens of withdrawals, just over the past few days. About $10,000 was gone. Karen's balance was zero. Her overdraft protection plan had automatically deducted another $1,200 from savings to cover the shortfall after the thief had cleaned out the checking account.

Karen filed a police report, closed her now-empty account and submitted a claim. With no money to cover checks, she couldn't pay her bills, her rent. She couldn't even buy groceries. Late fees were compounded by black marks on her credit report. And that was just the beginning.

*   *   *

At five-two and 110 pounds, Karen Lodrick was tiny compared with the nearly six-foot-tall woman carrying the brown suede coat. Block after block in downtown San Francisco, Karen chased the woman, keeping the 911 operator on the phone to let her know exactly where they were.

She lost sight of the woman after she turned a corner. But as Karen looked through the French doors leading into a stately old apartment building, there she was again. One glance at Karen and the woman took off down the hill toward Market Street, a main thoroughfare with multiple lanes in either direction.

Traffic whizzed by. Locals strolled the tree-lined sidewalks and walked in and out of funky coffeehouses. Some, toting bags of bottles and aluminum cans, meandered toward the recycling center. People of every description moved along Market Street. But she didn't see any police officers.

As the identity thief passed an abandoned shopping cart, Karen saw her arm swing out. She tossed something inside. Karen raced to the cart. "I got what she dropped," she told the 911 operator. "It's a wallet. A Prada wallet." Karen wanted to look inside, but she had no time.

The thief ran into a busy intersection against the light and flagged down a taxi. Karen panicked. "She is not going to get away," she cried to the operator. "I am not going to let her escape." She caught the taxi before the driver pulled out.

"Don't let her go!" she implored. "She's an identity thief." The driver lifted his hands off the wheel and held them up. Her escape thwarted, the woman got out and confronted Karen.

"Why are you chasing me?"

For an instant, Karen felt doubt. What if this wasn't the thief? She tried to convince the woman to wait for the police. But she took off down Market Street again, toward Octavia, where the freeway spilled out its traffic. Karen kept after her.

A vintage orange streetcar pulled up to the bus stop, and the woman jumped aboard, Karen right behind. Adrenaline pumping, she was totally focused on the thief.

"Please don't drive away," Karen told the driver. The thief

quickly ducked off again. "Why don't you just wait and you can talk to the police?" Karen called.

To Karen's surprise, the woman answered, saying she was on probation and would be arrested. Karen now had no doubt she'd found the right person.

* * *

It drove Karen crazy that it took about two weeks for the bank's credit card division to process the problem and recredit money to her account. She felt hopeful when the bank called to tell her it had a surveillance video of the thief. On it Karen saw a big, dark-haired woman in a suede coat and designer sunglasses at an ATM. Karen signed an affidavit that she didn't know the woman, got a printout of her image, and that was it.

Meanwhile, the thief reached deeper into Karen's life. She used her Social Security number and other information to get a counterfeit driver's license, showing Karen's license number but the thief's picture. With the license and the Social Security number, she reopened accounts that Karen had closed years before.

One day, the Dell computer company called Karen to confirm that it was all right to send "her" $7,000 order to an address different from the one on her account.

"Close that account and don't deliver those computers," she told Dell's rep, explaining someone had stolen her identity. She asked for the address the thief had wanted the equipment sent to. Dell refused to give her the address, saying she'd have to put the request in writing.

Karen placed fraud alerts with the credit reporting agencies. But that didn't stop the thief from opening more accounts in Karen's name. Again and again, she asked the bank to put an alert on her account, but when she checked, it wasn't there. The thief got into her new bank account, and the whole cycle began again. She was at her wit's end.

To add to her frustration, the bank claimed Karen had failed to come in to view the surveillance video. It didn't matter that she'd signed an affidavit. The bank couldn't find it and cut off access to her funds. She viewed the video again and signed another affidavit. The bank lost that one too. She signed another.

Now, with a phony driver's license, the thief was stalking her third checking account.

*   *   *

For half an hour, up and down the streets, around corners and into alleyways, Karen Lodrick, frightened but determined, pursued the woman with the suede coat. Karen lost her twice when she slipped into buildings to hide. And then she lost her a third time at an indoor parking lot. "It's over," she told the 911 operator. Exasperated and exhausted, Karen zipped open the Prada wallet.

Two of her bank statements were tucked into one side of the large wallet. On the other were the two debit cards used to clean out her account in November. She also found one of her own paychecks. But what chilled her most were tiny "cue cards" with her name, Social Security number, driver's license number and address.

The 911 operator assured her that an officer would be there as soon as he finished an emergency call, and Karen agreed to wait by the entrance to the garage. When the cop arrived a few minutes later, Karen told him what had occurred, feeling little hope that he'd find the woman now.

But only moments later, the officer found her—crouched between a car and the building, smoking a cigarette.

"Idiot! You should have kept running," Karen told her.

*   *   *

The arresting officer said the identity thief, Maria Nelson, had at least 60 prior arrests, was indeed on probation and was wanted in another jurisdiction for similar crimes. When Nelson came before a judge 44 days later, however, thanks to a plea deal with the prosecutor, she was sentenced to only time served plus probation.

Meanwhile, Karen keeps getting billed for phone service and items at a department store that she didn't buy. And she fears her ID may have been sold on the black market, prolonging her nightmare.

Karen Lodrick received unexpected bills for a couple more years. She is now working as a cyber security specialist and is an advocate for victims of identity theft.

HOUSE OF CARDS

by John Colapinto
from *Vanity Fair*

On August 22, 2015, Boye Brogeland posted a provocative comment to the website Bridgewinners.com. "Very soon there will come out mind-boggling stuff," wrote the Norwegian bridge player, then age 43 and ranked 64th in the world. "It will give us a tremendous momentum to clean the game up."

A few days later, Brogeland launched his own website, Bridgecheaters.com. The home page featured a huge photo of Lotan Fisher and Ron Schwartz, a young Israeli duo who, since breaking into the international ranks in 2011, had snapped up the game's top trophies. They appeared under the tagline "The greatest scam in the history of bridge!"

Brogeland posted examples of what he claimed to be suspiciously illogical hands played by the pair. He also laid out a pattern of alleged cheating and bad sportsmanship going as far back as 2003, when Fisher and Schwartz were in their mid-teens.

For the game of contract bridge, it was an earthquake equal to the jolt that shook international cycling when Lance Armstrong was banned from competition for doping. Fisher and Schwartz denied all wrongdoing and hired lawyers who dispatched a letter to Brogeland threatening a lawsuit and offering to settle if he paid them $1 million. In a message he denies was intended for Brogeland, Ron Fisher posted to his Facebook page: "Jealousy made you sick. Get ready for a meeting with the devil."

* * *

Brogeland lives in Flekkefjord, Norway, with his wife, Tonje, and their two young children. Having learned bridge at the age of eight from his grandparents, he fell in love with the game and turned pro at 28. In 2013, he was recruited by his current sponsor, Richie Schwartz (no relation to Ron), a Bronx-born bridge addict who made a fortune at the racetrack in the 1970s. Brogeland says Richie Schwartz pays him travel expenses and a base yearly salary of $50,000—with big bonuses for strong showings in tournaments.

Not long after Brogeland joined Richie Schwartz's team, he learned that his employer was also hiring Fisher and Ron Schwartz, about whom he had heard misgivings from other players. Over the next two years, Brogeland and his five teammates won a string of championships.

Nevertheless, Brogeland says he was relieved when, in the summer of 2015, Fisher and Ron Schwartz were lured away by Jimmy Cayne, former CEO of the defunct investment house Bear Stearns. "When they changed teams," Brogeland says, "I didn't have to be faced with this kind of environment where you feel something is strange but you can't really tell."

Fisher, meanwhile, was enjoying his position at the top of the game, where the lives of many successful young pros resemble those of globe-hopping rock musicians. Convening nightly at a hotel bar in whatever city is holding the competition—Biarritz, Chennai, Chicago—they drink until the small hours. Charismatic and darkly handsome, Fisher posted Instagram photos of himself in well-cut suits, behind the wheel of luxury cars or partying with an array of people.

There was only one problem: the persistent rumors that he

was a cheater. "But it's an unwritten rule that you do not publicly accuse anyone—even if you're sure," says Steve Weinstein, a top American player. It was a catch-22 that Fisher seemed to delight in flaunting, shrugging off questions about his suspicious play. "He had the Nietzschean superman personality," says Fred Gitelman, a professional player who has won championships worldwide. "He just thought he was in a different league."

∗ ∗ ∗

Contract bridge is built on the rules of the 18th-century British card game whist. Four people play in two-person partnerships. The player to the dealer's left leads with a card of any suit, and each player in succession plays a card of the suit led; the highest card wins the trick.

It's a simple game, slightly complicated by the existence of the trump: a card in a suit that overrules all others. In whist, trump is determined randomly. In auction bridge, a game popularized in England in 1904, each hand has an opening "auction," where the teams, communicating solely by way of *spoken* bids, establish which (if any) suit will be trump and how many tricks they think they can take. Pairs who take more tricks than contracted for are awarded extra points.

Contract bridge emerged from refinements American railroad magnate Harold S. Vanderbilt introduced in 1925. He sought to spice up auction bridge by awarding escalating bonus points to pairs who took the greatest risk in the opening auction, and imposed steep point deductions on those who failed to make the tricks contracted for. Thus did a polite British parlor game take on some of the sweaty-palmed excitement of the big-money trading of Wall Street.

The American Contract Bridge League (ACBL), the game's governing body in North America, lists only 168,000 members, with a median age (despite the hotel-bar set) of 71.

Yet the professional tournament game is a serious pursuit, with wealthy enthusiasts assembling stables of top players, paying them retainers and bonuses—all for the privilege of playing hands with the pros in important tournaments. With six world championships under her belt, Gail Greenberg, one of the game's greatest female champions, says that such pay-days have fueled cheating by players hoping to be recruited by deep-pocketed sponsors, or to hang onto the one they've got.

Pairs are forbidden to say what high cards they hold or in what suit they might be strong—except by way of the koan-like bids ("Two no trump"). Any other communication is out-lawed. In one of the game's biggest scandals, British champion J. Terence Reese and his partner, Boris Schapiro, were discov-ered in 1965 using finger signals to communicate the number of hearts they held.

Tournament organizers would eventually respond by erect-ing screens to block partners' view of each other. When play-ers were discovered communicating via footsie, barriers were installed under tables. Pairs can come under suspicion even when no signaling is detected.

"In bridge at the highest level," says Chris Willenken, a leading American professional, "the best players play in a relentlessly logical fashion, so when something illogical hap-pens, other good players notice it. And if that illogical thing is consistently winning, suspicions can be aroused."

*   *   *

Less than a month after Lotan Fisher and Ron Schwartz had left Richie Schwartz's team, Brogeland met the pair as oppo-nents, in the quarter-final of the 2015 Spingold at the Hilton hotel in Chicago. Brogeland's team was the clear underdog, but it won by the slimmest margin possible: a single point.

Or it seemed to. Fisher immediately contested the result on a technicality. After an arbitration that stretched until 1:30 a.m., the win was overturned: Brogeland's team had now lost by one point and been knocked out of the tournament.

That night, a crushed Brogeland could not sleep. He rose at 7 a.m. and opened Bridge Base Online (BBO), a website that archives tournament hands, to see exactly how he had lost. He immediately noticed something odd. Ron Schwartz had opened a hand by playing a club lead. Yet, Schwartz's hand indicated that a heart lead was the obvious play.

Then, he says, he saw something even stranger. In one of the hands, Fisher had claimed 11 tricks. Except Fisher, as BBO showed, held the cards for just 10 tricks. Brogeland thought it was a mistake and immediately contacted his sponsor. In any event, challenges must be raised within a half-hour of a match. The loss would stand.

* * *

Brogeland spent the next two days at the tournament scouring BBO and comparing notes with other players. By the time he flew back to Norway, he was convinced Fisher and Schwartz were signaling to each other, but he had no idea how. Still, he believed that if he amassed enough illogical hands, he could make a convincing case, however circumstantial.

Brogeland contacted governing bodies on both sides of the Atlantic. When he gave suspect hands to the ACBL, he was told to supply more. "They had plenty of hands," he says. "Fifty, 60. I said, 'How many do you need? One hundred? Two hundred? Please do something!'"

Robert Hartman, the CEO of ACBL, declines to discuss the specifics of ongoing investigations but admits that the process for reviewing cheating can take a year or longer to play out.

Fisher and Schwartz aren't the only pair suspected of cheating in recent history, either. Fulvio Fantoni and Claudio Nunes of Italy—ranked first and second in the world in the 2014 European Championships—have also been reported to the ACBL by a colleague, and an investigation into allegations against the pair is still pending.

For his part, Brogeland had no intention of waiting. Despite the risks to his career and reputation—not to mention the fact that he would be challenging rich and powerful interests—he decided to bypass the official channels and go public. And so, on August 28, 2015 he went live with Bridge Cheaters, where he laid out his evidence.

Experienced cheating investigators were underwhelmed. Kit Woolsey, a mathematician who has previously done statistical analyses for the ACBL to help implicate cheaters, wrote on Bridge Winners, "His example hands are an indication of possible wrongdoing, but I do not believe that by themselves they are proof of anything."

Barry Goren, a U.S. professional, excoriated Brogeland for publicly accusing the pair without due process. "Personally," Goren wrote on Bridge Winners, "I think Boye should be thrown out of bridge for the way this was handled."

As if in tacit acknowledgement of how his failure to uncover actual signaling by Fisher and Schwartz weakened his case, Brogeland had included links to three YouTube videos of the pair in match play. On August 30, 2015, Brogeland's friend Per-Ola Cullin, a semi-professional bridge player, watched one of the videos. In it, Fisher makes a suspicious heart lead.

Cullin noticed that Schwartz set down the small slotted board that holds the cards. This was normal. But he didn't place the board in the center of the table, its usual spot. Instead he slid it a few inches to the right, to one side of the opening in the trapdoor of the anti-cheating screen. Cullin decided to watch the previous hand. The board had been positioned in the same peculiar spot—but this time by Fisher. As with the succeeding hand, the team led hearts. "My adrenalin started pumping," Cullin says. "I started watching all the matches from the European championships."

After several hours, Cullin was convinced the board's placement signaled what suit the partner should lead with. At a little after 3 a.m., he texted Brogeland, who forwarded the information to Woolsey.

Three days later, Woolsey posted to Bridge Winners an essay entitled "The Videos Speak," confirming Cullin's hypothesis. Fisher and Schwartz were suspended by the ACBL and placed under investigation by that body and the European Bridge League (EBL). It was an extraordinary exoneration for Brogeland. But he wasn't done yet.

* * *

Maaijke Mevius, a 45-year-old living in the Netherlands, is a physicist and an avid recreational bridge player. Galvanized by the evidence against Fisher and Schwartz, she wondered if *she* could spot any illegal signaling in YouTube videos. While watching Fantoni and Nunes, she grew convinced she had decoded how they were using card placement to signal to their partner whether they held any high honor cards (ace, king or queen). Mevius e-mailed the information to Brogeland.

On September 13, 2015, Bridge Winners published "The Videos Speak: Fantoni-Nunes," a damning analysis by Woolsey. In a statement from that month, the pair said, "We will not comment on allegations at this time."

On Bridge Winners, the first reader comment in response to this news said it all: "Is this the end? Speechless now . . ."

* * *

It wasn't quite the end. Brogeland soon received an anonymous e-mail tip from someone identifying himself as "No Matter." The tipster advised looking at videos of Germany's Alex Smirnov and Josef Piekarek, as well as the Polish pair Cezary Balicki and Adam Zmudzinski. In subsequent e-mails, No Matter pointed out what to watch for: signaling based on where the pair put the special bidding cards in the bidding tray that is passed between the players during the auction.

Smirnov and Piekarek, told of the discovery, admitted to the violation in a statement. Balicki and Zmudzinski denied the charges.

Still more astonishing, however, is the fact that Brogeland believes the person behind the mask of No Matter is the disgraced Lotan Fisher.

Brogeland cannot explain why Fisher would assist in the quest to root out cheaters—unless, by helping to expose others, he hoped to take the focus off himself. Fisher, in an e-mail to this writer, claims that he only aided No Matter and that his motivation was the same as Brogeland's—to clean up the game. "I love [bridge] more than Boye or anyone else," he wrote, adding, "My next step is to prove that me and Ron Schwartz didn't cheat. NEVER."

* * *

In May, Bridge Winners announced that the EBL had issued Fisher and Schwartz a five-year ban from its events and a lifetime ban on playing as partners. The other pairs have also faced repercussions from various leagues and events.

Brogeland's actions have also had a more permanent effect on the game. In December 2015, the ACBL held one of bridge's biggest annual tournaments, the American nationals. For the first time, the ACBL had installed small video cameras and microphones at the tables to record all matches from the quarter-finals through to the finals—since no one imagines that every dishonest pair has been rooted out.

Before the end of the tournament, ACBL CEO Hartman convened the first meeting of a new anti-cheating task force—including Willenken, Woolsey and Cullin—who discussed means for streamlining the process of submitting complaints and investigating them.

Meanwhile, the International Bridge Press Association named Brogeland the Bridge Personality of the Year for 2015. When he arrived for his first match at the Denver nationals last autumn, he had to fight his way through the crowd that had collected outside the tournament room. "Thank you for your service," said a bearded man who had stopped Brogeland at the door of the game room.

"Well, I had to do it," Brogeland said, shaking the man's hand and trying to move off.

"You really put yourself on the line," the man persisted.

Brogeland smiled. "Bridge deserves it," he said, then headed for his table.

Lotan Fisher and Ron Schwartz were expelled from the ACBL in 2016. Fulvio Fantoni and Claudio Nunes were suspended from the ACBL and the EBL and banned from playing as partners. Josef Piekarek and Alex Smirnov were suspended from the EBL and ACBL until 2020 and banned from playing together for life. In 2017, Cezary Balicki and Adam Zmudzinski were prohibited from playing in the Polish Bridge Union until further notice.

HOW WE TRAPPED CAPONE

by Frank J. Wilson,
former chief, U.S. Secret Service,
as told to Howard Whitman

When my wife and I left Baltimore for Chicago in 1928, all I said was, "Judith, I'm after a fellow named Curly Brown." If I'd told her that Curly Brown was an alias of Scarface Al Capone, she'd have turned the car around then and there and made me take up some respectable trade like piano tuning. My assignment was to find clear proof of income-tax evasion by Capone. In previous years he had filed no tax return or had reported insignificant income.

Art Madden, our Chicago agent-in-charge, told me that hanging an income-tax rap on Alphonse Capone would be as easy as hanging a foreclosure sign on the moon. The Grand Panjandrum of the checkered suits and diamond belts had Cook County in the palm of his hand. He did all his business anonymously, through front men. To discourage meddlers, his production department was turning out fifty corpses a year.

For a base of operations the government gave me and my three assistants an overgrown closet in the old Post Office Building, with a cracked glass at the door, no windows, a double flat-topped desk and peeling walls. I spent months in fruitless investigation through banks, credit agencies and newspaper files.

I prowled the crummy streets of Cicero but could get no clue to show that a dollar from the big gambling places, the horse parlors, the brothels or bootleg joints ever reached Scarface Al Capone. Jake Lingle, a Chicago *Tribune* reporter, had been seen with Capone in Chicago and Miami and, from the tips I got, he wasn't just writing interviews. So I saw the *Tribune* boss, Robert R. McCormick, and told him Jake Lingle's help would be appreciated by the United States government. "I'll get word to Lingle to go all the way with you," said the colonel. Lingle was assassinated next day in a subway, right in the busiest part of the city.

I was stuck, bogged down. Sixteen frustrating months dragged by. Capone was all over the front pages every day. It was common talk that he got a cut on every case of whiskey brought into Cook County; that he ran a thousand speakeasies, a thousand bookie joints, fifteen gambling houses, a string of brothels; that he controlled half a dozen breweries. He had brought a Florida palace on Palm Island and was spending $1000 a week on banquets. He tore around in sixteen-cylinder limousines, slept in fifty-dollar pajamas and ordered fifteen suits at a time at $135 each. His personal armed forces numbered seven hundred, equipped with automatic weapons and armored automobiles. But evidence of lavish living wasn't enough. The courts had to see *income*.

One night, in a desperate mood, I decided to check over all the data which my three assistants and I had piled up. By one o'clock in the morning I was bleary-eyed, and while gathering up my papers I accidentally bumped into our filing cabinet. It clicked shut. I couldn't find the key anywhere. Now where'll I put this stuff? I wondered. Just outside, in a neighboring storeroom, I found an old filing cabinet full of dusty envelopes. I can lay this old junk on the table, I thought to myself. I'll put my own stuff in overnight.

In the back of the cabinet was a heavy package tied in brown paper. Just out of curiosity I snipped the string and found three ledgers, one a "special column cashbook." My eye leaped over the column headings: "Bird cage," "21," "Craps," "Faro," "Roulette," "Horse bets." Here was the diary of a large operation, with a take from $20,000 to $30,000 a day. Net profits were for only eighteen months (the books were dated 1925–26) were over half a million dollars.

"Who could have run a mill that size?" I asked myself. The answer hit me like a baseball bat: only three people—Frankie Lake, Terry Druggan or Al Capone! But I had already cleaned up the Druggan-Lake case. Two from three leaves one.

The ledgers had been picked up in a raid after the murder of Assistant State's Attorney William McSwiggin in 1926. They came from one of the biggest gambling palaces in Cicero, The Ship, where diamond-studded crowds from Chicago laid down $3,000,000 a year in wagers. Here was a record of *income*. If I could hang it around the neck of Al Capone, we'd have a case at last.

Scarface must have found out that we were closing in. On the inside of the gang I had planted one of the best undercover men I have ever known, Eddie O'Hare. One afternoon word reached me that Eddie wanted to see me at once. When we met, he was red-faced and excited. "You've got to move out of your hotel, Frank. The big fellow has brought in four killers from New York to get you. They know where they keep your automobile and what time you come in and go out. You've got to get out this afternoon!"

"Thanks for tipping me off, Eddie," I replied. So I phoned Judith I had a surprise for her—we were moving to the Palmer House, where she had once said she'd like to live. I left word at my hotel we were going to Kansas and drove to the Union

Station—but right on through and around to Palmer. Judith was completely confused and I hoped Al's torpedoes were, too.

Later Eddie met me with another report: "The big fellow's offering $25,000 reward to anybody who bumps you off!" When the story broke in the papers that Capone had put a price on my head, Judith took it with amazing calm. She simply said, "We're going straight home to Baltimore!" I finally won her over by promising she could be with me as much as possible. Women always think they're bulletproof.

Meanwhile I was working on the handwriting in the ledgers of The Ship. I think we must have collected handwriting samples of every hoodlum in Chicago—from voting registers, savings accounts, police courts. The painful process of elimination finally left me with a character named Lou Shumway, whose writing on a bank deposit slip was a dead twin to that in the ledgers. I heard from a tipster that Shumway was in Miami, probably working at Hialeah or the dog tracks. All I had to go on was a description: "Shumway is a perfect little gentleman, refined, slight, harmless—not a racetrack sport at all."

In February 1931, I stood by the rail at Hialeah looking at the man I had been stalking for nearly three years. Scarface Al Capone sat in a box with a jeweled moll on either side of him, smoking a long cigar, greeting a parade of fawning sycophants who came to shake his hand. I looked upon his pudgy olive face, his thick pursed lips, the rolls of fat descending from his chin—and the scar, like a heavy pencil line across his cheek. When a country constable wants a man, I thought, he just walks up and says, "You're pinched." Here I was, with the whole U.S. government behind me, as powerless as a canary.

Two nights later, I spotted the "perfect little gentleman" my tipster had described, working at a dog track. I tailed him home, and picked him up next morning as he was having breakfast with this wife. He turned pale green. When I got him to the Federal Building, I said cold-turkey: "I am investigating the income-tax liability of one Alphonse Capone."

Gentleman Lou turned greener yet, but he pulled himself together and said, "Oh, you're mistaken. I don't know Al Capone."

I put my hand on his shoulder. "Lou," I said, "you have only two choices: If you refuse to play ball with me, I will send a deputy marshal to look for you at the track, ask for you by name and serve a summons on you. You get the point, Lou. As soon as the gang knows the government has located you, they will probably decide to bump you off so you can't testify.

"If you don't like that idea, Lou, come clean. Tell the truth about these ledgers. You were bookkeeper at The Ship. You can identify every entry in these books—and you can tell who your boss was. I'll guarantee to keep it secret until the day of the trial that you are playing ball with me. You will be guarded day and night, and I'll guarantee that Mrs. Shumway will not become a widow." Lou quivered like a harp string but finally gave in. I spirited him out of Miami and hid him in California.

But we still had to show that *income* actually reached the pockets of Al Capone. A painstaking checkup on all the recorded money transactions in Cicero finally showed that one "J.C. Dunbar" had brought gunnysacks full of cash to the Pinkert State Bank and bought $300,000 in cashier's checks.

Agent Nels Tessem and I caught up with "Dunbar," whose real name was Fred Ries, in St. Louis. We tailed a messenger boy with a special-delivery letter and slapped a subpoena in Ries's palm. He was annoyed, especially since the letter was from Capone's headquarters telling him to flee to Mexico. He wouldn't talk at first. But after a week in a special vermin-ridden cell in jail we picked out for him—we knew he had a pathological fear of bugs—Ries cried uncle. We sneaked him before a Chicago grand jury in the middle of the night. His testimony put the profits of The Ship squarely in the pockets of Scarface Al! I packed my scowling little treasure off to South America with government agents to guard him until we should need him in court.

In the autumn of 1931, two weeks before the Capone trial, Eddie O'Hare reported to me: "Capone's boys have a complete list of the prospective jurors. They're fixing them one by one—passing out thousand-dollar bills, promising political jobs, giving donations to churches. They're using muscle, too, Frank." Eddie handed me a list of ten names and addresses. "They're right off the jury list—names 30 to 39!"

Next morning I went with U.S. Attorney George E. Q. Johnson to the chambers of Federal Judge James H. Wilkerson, who was to sit in the Capone trial. The judge was reassuring— somehow he seemed like a match for Scarface Al. Sure enough, the ten names Eddie had given me tallied with the judge's list. But the judge didn't seem ruffled. He said calmly, "Bring your case into court as planned, gentlemen. Leave the rest to me."

The day the trial started, I fought my way through reporters, photographers and sob sisters. Al Capone came into the courtroom in a mustard-colored suit and sat down at the counsel table just a few feet from me. Phil D'Andrea, Al's favorite bodyguard, sat beside him, sneering at the crowd. As Judge Wilkerson entered in his black robe, Capone, behind the mask of his moonface, seemed to be snickering over the jury of newfound friends and intimidees who would soon send him back to the overlordship of Chicago.

Judge Wilkerson called his bailiff to the bench. He said in crisp, low tones, "Judge Edwards has another trial commencing today. Go to his courtroom and bring me his panel of jurors.

Take my entire panel to Judge Edwards." The switch was so smooth, so simple. Capone's face clouded with the black despair of a gambler who had made his final raise—and lost.

The trial marched on. My gems, Gentleman Lou Shumway and the bug-bedeviled Ries, stood their ground on the witness stand, though Capone and Phil D'Andrea were staring holes through them the entire time. I kept my eyes on D'Andrea. When he got up to stretch during a recess I could have sworn I saw a bulge in his right hip pocket. But no, I thought, there wasn't a crumb in the world who would dare to bring a gun into federal court. I saw him stretch again. I had the boys send in word that a reporter wanted to see him. I followed him out of the courtroom. Nels Tesem and Jay Sullivan, my colleagues, led him down the corridor. As we passed Judge Wilkerson's chamber I shoved him inside. "Give me that gun!" I snapped. D'Andrea handed it over. "Give me those bullets!" He ladled out a handful of ammunition.

Judge Wilkerson interrupted the trial to cite D'Andrea for contempt and send him away for six months. Capone growled, "I don't care what happens to D'Andrea. He's a damn fool. I don't care if he gets ten years." Al was cracking.

The trial wound up in mid-October. As the jury returned I felt sure we had won. "Gentlemen," intoned Judge Wilkerson, "what is your verdict?"

"Guilty!" The courtroom broke up like a circus after the last performance. Reporters ran out of court. Lawyers ran. Mobsters ran. Everybody seemed to be running but Scarface Al Capone. He slumped forward as if a blackjack had hit him.

When I got home, Judith cried, "You did it! I knew you were going to do it all the time!" Then she sighed. "Now can we go back to Baltimore?"

THE MAN WHO RIGGED THE LOTTERY

by Reid Forgrave
from the *New York Times Magazine*

The video was grainy, but it showed enough to possibly crack open the biggest lottery scam in American history. A heavyset man walks into a QuikTrip convenience store just off Interstate 80 in Des Moines, Iowa, two days before Christmas 2010. The hood of his sweatshirt is pulled over his head, obscuring his face. He grabs a fountain drink and two hot dogs.

"Hello!" the cashier says brightly.

Head down, the man replies in a low-pitched drawl: "Hell-ooooh."

They exchange a few more words. The man pulls two pieces of paper from his pocket. The cashier runs them through the lottery terminal and then hands over some change. Once outside, the man pulls off his hood, gets into his SUV, and drives away.

The pieces of paper were play slips for Hot Lotto, a lottery game that was available in 14 states and Washington, DC. A player (or the game's computer) picked five numbers and then a sixth, known as the Hot Ball. Players who got all six numbers right won a jackpot that varied according to how many tickets were sold. At the time of the video, the jackpot was approaching $10 million. The stated odds of winning it were 1 in 10,939,383.

Six days later, on December 29, the Hot Lotto numbers were selected: 3, 12, 16, 26, 33, 11. The next day, the Iowa Lottery announced that a QuikTrip in Des Moines had sold the winning ticket. But no one came forward to claim the now $16.5 million jackpot.

After a month passed, the Iowa Lottery held a news conference to note that the money was still uncollected. The lottery issued another public reminder three months after the winning numbers were announced, then another at six months and again at nine months, each time warning that winners had one year to claim their money.

In November 2011, a man named Philip Johnston, a Canadian attorney, called in with the correct serial number from the winning ticket. But when asked what he'd been wearing when he bought it, his description of a sports coat and gray flannel dress pants did not match the QuikTrip video. Then, in a subsequent call, the man admitted he had "fibbed"; he said he was helping a client claim the ticket so the client wouldn't be identified.

This was against the Iowa Lottery rules, which require identities of winners to be public. Lottery officials were suspicious: The winner's anonymity was worth $16.5 million?

"I was convinced it would never be claimed," says Mary Neubauer, the Iowa Lottery's vice president of external relations, of the jackpot.

And it wasn't, until exactly a year after the drawing—less than two hours before the 4 p.m. deadline—when representatives from a Des Moines law firm showed up at lottery headquarters with the winning ticket. The firm was claiming the prize on behalf of a trust whose beneficiary was a corporation in Belize. Its president was Philip Johnston—the same man who said he'd worn a sports coat to buy the ticket.

"It just absolutely stank all over the place," says Terry Rich, chief executive of the Iowa Lottery. So they held on to the jackpot while the attorney general's office opened an investigation. But it went nowhere.

*   *   *

Two years later, a baby-faced district attorney named Rob Sand inherited the languishing lottery file. In college, Sand had studied computer coding before going to law school, where his specialty was white-collar crime. Still, this case stumped him. His best evidence was that grainy video of a man in a hoodie, so he decided to release the footage to the media, hoping it might spark leads—and it did.

The first came from an employee of the Maine Lottery who recognized the distinct voice in the video as that of a man who had conducted a security audit in their offices. A web developer at the Iowa Lottery also recognized the voice: It belonged to a man she had worked alongside for years, Eddie Tipton. Eddie was the information-security director for the Multi-State Lottery Association, based in Des Moines. Among the games the association ran: the Hot Lotto.

*   *   *

Eddie cut a big figure around the lottery office. He wrote software, handled network firewalls, and reviewed security for games in nearly three dozen states. His life revolved around his job; he sometimes stayed at his desk until 11 p.m. When a coworker was in a bad mood, one colleague said, Eddie would pat him on the shoulder and say, "I just want you to know I'm your friend."

But he was also a paranoid sort. He rarely paid with credit cards, worried about people tracing his identity. In private moments, Eddie told friends he was lonely and wanted a family more than anything. He built a 4,800-square-foot, $540,000 house in the cornfields south of Des Moines, complete with five bedrooms and a stadium-style home theater. Friends wondered why a single man needed such a big house and how he could afford it on his salary. Eddie told them he had poured his savings into the house in hopes of filling it with a wife and children. But the right partner never came along.

Among Eddie's friends was a colleague named Jason Maher. They spent hours playing the online game World of Tanks. When Maher saw the Hot Lotto video that DA Sand released, Maher immediately recognized that familiar, low-pitched voice, but he didn't want to believe it. "That night I sat down—there's no way Eddie did this," Maher says. "There's got to be something wrong."

So he did what a computer whiz does: He put the file into audio software, removed the white noise, and isolated the voice. Then he took footage from security cameras in his own house—Eddie had just visited the night before—and compared the voices. "It was a complete and utter match," Maher said. The next day, he went to the QuikTrip and measured the dimensions of the tiles on the floor, the height of the shelving units, the distance between the door and the cash register. He used the results to compare the hand size, foot size, and height of the man in the video with his friend's. Maher wanted to be able to tell law enforcement that it wasn't his pal Eddie. "Once I did this, it was like, 'Well, [expletive]—it's Eddie.'"

* * *

In January 2015, state investigators showed up at Eddie's office. He was arrested and charged with two felony counts of fraud. Half a year later, on a hot, sticky July morning, Rob Sand stood before a jury at the Polk County Courthouse. "This is a classic story about an inside job," he began. "A man who by virtue of his employment is not allowed to play the lottery—nor allowed to win—buys a lottery ticket, wins, and passes the ticket along to be claimed by someone unconnected to him."

The prosecution knew Eddie had bought the winning ticket—the video made that pretty clear. So did cell phone records, which showed Eddie was in town that day, not out of town for the holidays as he had claimed. Investigators believed he'd fixed the lottery. But if the numbers are supposed to be generated randomly, how did he do it?

Based on his research, Sand theorized that before the Hot Lotto jackpot, Eddie had managed to gain access to one of the two computers that select the winning numbers and inserted a thumb drive containing a string of coded instructions he'd written. The clandestine software, called a rootkit, allowed Eddie to restrict the pool of numbers that could hit—and then it deleted itself.

The prosecutor told the jury members that they didn't have to understand the exact technology to convict Eddie. They just had to realize the near-impossible coincidence of the lottery security chief's buying the winning ticket. After deliberating for only five hours, the jury found Eddie guilty. He appealed.

Then the case took a very strange turn.

* * *

One morning a few months after the original trial, Sand's office phone rang. The call came from area code 281, in Texas, where Eddie grew up. The caller said he'd seen an article in the newspaper about Eddie's conviction. "Did y'all know," the tipster asked, "that Eddie's brother Tommy Tipton won the lottery, maybe about ten years back?"

Sand contacted Richard Rennison, a special agent at the FBI office in Texas City, Texas. Rennison said he remembered the case well: In 2006, a man named Tom Bargas had contacted local law enforcement with a suspicious story. Bargas owned 44 fireworks stands. Twice a year—after the Fourth of July and New Year's—he handled enormous amounts of cash. A man he knew, a local justice of the peace, called Bargas around New Year's and said, "I got half a million in cash that I want to swap with your money."

What's a justice of the peace who makes around $35,000 a year doing with that much cash? Bargas thought. Suspicious, he called the police, who called the FBI. Soon, agents listened in as Bargas met with the justice of the peace, Tommy Tipton. Tommy pulled out a briefcase filled with $450,000 in cash, still in Federal Reserve wrappers, and swapped $100,000 of it for Bargas's worn, circulated bills. The FBI then went to work investigating the serial numbers on the new bills.

A few months later, Rennison went to see Tommy. He said that he had hit the lottery but was on the outs with his wife and trying to keep the winnings from her. A friend had claimed the $568,990 prize in exchange for 10 percent of the money. At the time, it all seemed to add up, and the Tommy Tipton case was closed.

Now Sand suspected that there were even more illicitly claimed tickets out there. He knew from experience that white-collar criminals aren't usually caught on their first attempt.

In fact, a $783,257.72 jackpot from a Wisconsin Lottery drawing on December 29, 2007, had been claimed by a Texas man named Robert Rhodes—Eddie Tipton's best friend. On November 23, 2011, Kyle Conn from Hemphill, Texas, won $644,478 in the Oklahoma Lottery. Sand saw that Tommy

Tipton had three Facebook friends named Conn. He got a list of possible phone numbers and cross-referenced them with Tommy's cell phone records. Another hit.

Two winning Kansas Lottery tickets with $15,402 payouts were purchased on December 23, 2010—the day Eddie bought the Iowa ticket. Cell phone records indicated he was driving through Kansas on the way to Texas for the holidays. One of the winning tickets was claimed by a Texan named Christopher McCoulskey; the other, by an Iowan named Amy Warrick. Each was a friend of Eddie's.

One morning, Sand and an investigator knocked on Warrick's door. She told them Eddie had said he wasn't able to claim a winning lottery ticket because of his job. If she could claim it, he'd said, she could keep a portion as a gift for her recent engagement.

"You have these honest dupes," Sand says. "All these people are being offered thousands of dollars for doing something that's a little bit sneaky but not illegal." Investigators in Iowa now had six tickets they figured were part of a bigger scam. But the question remained: How did it work?

* * *

Fortunately, the computers used in the 2007 Wisconsin Lottery jackpot were sitting in storage. A computer expert, Sean McLinden, unearthed some malicious computer code. It hadn't been hidden; you just needed to know what to look for.

"This," says Wisconsin assistant attorney general David Maas, "was finding the smoking gun."

Eddie Tipton pleaded guilty, as did his brother, Tommy. Now facing ten years in prison, Eddie agreed to spill his secrets, which lottery officials hoped would help them safeguard the games in the future. He explained that the whole scheme had started fairly innocently one day when he walked past one of the accountants at the Multi-State Lottery Association. "Hey, did you put your secret numbers in there?" the accountant teased Eddie.

"What do you mean?"

"Well, you know, you can set numbers on any given day since you wrote the software."

"Just like a little seed that was planted," Eddie said. "And then during one slow period, I tried it."

To ensure that the winning numbers were generated randomly, the computer took a reading from a Geiger counter that measured radiation in the surrounding air. The radiation reading was plugged into an algorithm to come up with the winning lottery numbers.

Eddie's scheme was to limit the random selection process as much as possible. His code kicked in only if the coming drawing fulfilled a narrow set of circumstances. It had to be on a Wednesday or a Saturday evening, and one of three dates in a non–leap year: the 147th day of the year, the 327th day, or the 363rd day. Investigators noticed those dates generally fell around holidays—Memorial Day, Thanksgiving, and Christmas—when Eddie was often on vacation.

If those criteria were satisfied, the random-number generator was diverted to a different track that didn't use the Geiger counter reading. Instead, the algorithm ran with a predetermined number, which restricted the pool of potential winning numbers to a much smaller, predictable set of options: Rather than millions of possible winning combinations, there would be only a few hundred.

The night before the first lottery he rigged, a $4.8 million jackpot in Colorado, Eddie stayed late in his messy, computer-filled office. He set a test computer to run the program over and over again and wrote down all the potential winning numbers on a yellow legal pad.

The next day, November 23, 2005, he handed the pad to his brother, who was headed to Colorado on a trip. "These numbers have a good chance of winning based on my analysis," he said. "Play them. Play them all."

*   *   *

On a clear summer day in Des Moines last year, Eddie Tipton, who was then 54, trudged up the stairs of the Polk County Courthouse. His hands were shoved in his pockets, his head down. He had accepted a plea deal for masterminding the massive lottery scam—one count of ongoing criminal conduct, part of a package deal that gave his brother only 75 days. Eddie was here for his sentencing.

In statements to prosecutors, he painted himself as a kind of coding Robin Hood, stealing from the lottery and helping people in need: his brother, who had five daughters; his friend who'd just gotten engaged. "I didn't really need the money," Eddie said. The judge noted that Eddie seemed to rationalize his actions—that he didn't think it was necessarily illegal, just taking advantage of a hole in the system, sort of like counting cards at a casino.

The judge sentenced Eddie to a maximum of 25 years in prison. The brothers' restitution to the various state lotteries came to $2.2 million, even though, according to his attorney, Eddie himself pocketed only around $350,000.

Sand expects Eddie to be released on parole within seven years. Reflecting on the case, the prosecutor says he felt a deep intellectual satisfaction in solving the puzzle: "The justice system at its best is really about a search for truth."

I STARED DOWN DEATH

by Christopher W. Davis

Tammi Smith got up early and dressed in jeans and a white shirt. She had an appointment in traffic court in Shelbyville, Indiana, over a minor violation. Waking her husband, Shawn, with a kiss, she told him she was taking the van. The kids were already up, eating cereal and watching cartoons. After court, she thought she might stop to get her nails done and then pick up sodas at the Bigfoot convenience store on the way home.

Eighty miles down the interstate in Cincinnati, Ohio, Dennis McAninch and his friend Joseph G. Scalf also had appointments in court. On burglary charges. McAninch, a 34-year-old ex-con with multiple felony arrests and convictions, was currently out on parole after serving five years for burglary. But instead of showing for their court dates, the pair drove across the state line into Indiana in McAninch's 1999 white Ford compact.

In Batesville, an off-duty policeman noticed the car slowly cruising a neighborhood. There'd recently been a string of burglaries there—and this guy drove like someone casing houses. The officer called in a description of the vehicle, and in minutes a police car was on the scene, lights flashing.

McAninch pulled over and lifted his shirt, showing Scalf the 9 mm semiautomatic in his belt. He kept the engine running. Then, as the officer approached, he gunned it and took off.

* * *

Tammi's traffic case was quickly resolved without a fine. Leaving the courthouse, she checked her watch. She still had time to get her nails done.

* * *

McAninch reached speeds of up to 120 mph on Interstate 74, swerving around stop sticks on the highway and throwing screwdrivers, bottles, anything he could put his hands on, out the window at police.

* * *

After leaving the manicurist, Tammi drove east on Route 44 to Bigfoot. She pulled up to the front door of the convenience store. Intending to dash in and pick up some sodas, she left her keys and cell phone on the seat.

* * *

In his frantic attempt to escape, McAninch finally crashed into another vehicle, damaging his Ford, which barely made it off the highway into the Bigfoot lot. He leaped out of the car and dashed for the store as police cars pulled in, in close pursuit. Scalf held his hands out of the passenger window and surrendered. McAninch kept running, firing twice at police.

* * *

Tammi was at the register, holding a copy of the *Shelbyville News*, when a stocky man in a long-sleeved white shirt and jeans burst through the front door with a gun in his hand. "Everybody get out or I'm going to kill you!"

Two female employees rushed for the back door. McAninch leaped over the counter, cornering the clerk, a young man, at the register. Not knowing what to do, Tammi ducked behind a food rack at the back of the store.

But McAninch saw her. "You, get up here!" he shouted.

Okay, Tammi told herself, this is God's plan for me today. I might die. Don't be afraid of dying. Everybody's got their time. This might be mine.

*   *   *

As police cars gathered in the parking lot, McAninch ordered the clerk to lock the front door. The young man eased around the counter, locked the door and pocketed the key. Then, seeing McAninch was focused on the police out front, he bolted for the back door.

Tammi was now alone with the gunman.

McAninch grabbed her by the hair, forced her up to the window and put his gun to her head—showing police he had a hostage.

"Please don't shoot me," Tammi said. She started to cry. "I have kids."

McAninch turned the gun away and instead fired a shot through the window at police. Then he dragged Tammi to the back of the store and into a windowless office, a cramped space with a desk, two chairs, a phone and two computer monitors, one that showed views from security cameras inside the store.

McAninch told Tammi to take a seat and then sat next to her. The wait began. Tammi knew her only chance was to stay calm, show no emotion and try to keep talking to this guy.

The office phone began to ring. One of the calls was from a reporter at Indianapolis radio station WIBC, who had heard about the police chase and called for an eyewitness account.

McAninch told her he was holding a hostage, and then asked the reporter to call a woman friend. The reporter linked them on a conference call and later broadcast portions of their conversation.

"What's up, baby?" asked McAninch.

"Nothing," the woman responded. "What's wrong?"

"I'm in a gas station. There's about 50 police outside. I shot at them so . . . they're probably going to end up killing me."

She tried to talk sense to him. "Can't you go out with your hands up?" she asked. "Figure another way out of this."

Nothing changed his mind. In the midst of the conversation, McAninch even put Tammi on the phone.

As time dragged on, Tammi asked him if she could go to the bathroom, but McAninch said, "Baby, I just can't let you go up there. They're liable to shoot through the windows." Eventually he allowed her to relieve herself in a trash can.

At long last, police took command of the phone line. They now controlled McAninch's access to the outside world through a police negotiator.

When he first called, the negotiator asked McAninch who he was holding hostage. Was she all right? Did he or Tammi need medical attention? Then the negotiator settled into a long conversation calculated to keep McAninch calm.

Tammi was working on the same idea. When McAninch was off the phone, she took family photos out of her wallet. "Here's my daughter," she told him. "She's a cheerleader. She's ten. Isn't she beautiful?"

McAninch studied the photo. "Yeah, she's a beautiful girl."

"Do you have any kids?" Tammi asked.

Yes, he said, one, a 13-year-old daughter, but he had no pictures.

Tammi was trying to get to know him. Win his trust. It

was already obvious to her that he wasn't expecting to get out alive. She had to find a way to convince him not to take her with him.

*   *   *

In between phone calls, McAninch checked the layout of the store. The back entrance was a thick cold-storage door with a large metal handle. McAninch braced a stepladder against the handle and built a barricade of food boxes.

All the while, Tammi kept McAninch talking, looking for anything to engage him. He had tattoos running up the right side of his neck—his birth sign, Virgo. And on his right arm were two women's names; one was his daughter's. On his left arm, there was a poem for his parents. Tammi could only make out the last line: "Let there be no more tears." She stored it all away.

"Your daughter needs you," she said. "You know that."

"Yeah, I know," McAninch said.

"You need to give up," she said, keeping her tone even, trying not to sound bossy or pushy, more like a friend giving advice. She repeated what the police had earlier told him. "Give me the gun. Put it in a plastic bag. I'll carry it out." She kept talking. "Do your time, and you'll get out."

"I can't do that," he said.

*   *   *

There was money everywhere. Tammi had never seen a room so disorganized. There was cash piled on the desk in the office. Checks written out to Bigfoot all over the place. Bunches of cash behind the chairs. McAninch stuffed over $1,000 into his pockets. And handed Tammi $350 out of the stack of cash on the table.

"I can't take that," she told him. "God's watching. I'm not a thief."

"Take it," he insisted. "Put it in your wallet—now!"

She tried to shake him off. "All I want is to go home and make dinner for my family."

"I can't let you go. You're my security blanket," McAninch told her. "You're what's keeping me alive."

* * *

Emergency response teams (SWAT units) from state, county and city jurisdictions were now on the scene. Police put gunmen in place. A mobile command center had been set up some 500 yards from the store near the interstate overpass. The press corps had arrived en masse.

Alerted by the radio broadcast, Tammi's husband, Shawn, his parents and her mother and stepfather had rushed to the scene. A state police chaplain was assigned to stay with the family. Police told them Tammi was not hurt—and, in a convenience store, not hungry. They said they would do anything to keep her safe. One officer told the press, "We are prepared to talk until the last Ho Ho is gone."

* * *

Fifteen hours crept by. McAninch sat thinking, tapping the gun against his head and making multiple demands of the police negotiator. He wanted to visit his mother's grave before being locked up, he wanted his pal Joe Scalf set free, he wanted to talk to his daughter, he wanted a live television crew filming his surrender so there wouldn't be any monkey business, and he wanted cold beer. "Of all places to hold up," he said, "I chose one that doesn't sell beer."

Through it all, Tammi was close enough to him to grab his

gun, but even if she could wrestle it from him, she knew she'd never be able to use it. She tried to maintain an appearance of calm.

"You're a pretty cool hostage," he said, and told the police: "This bitch ain't scared at all."

Slowly McAninch began to talk to her. He confessed he was bipolar. That he used Valium. He had marijuana with him and started to smoke a joint, offering her a puff. She said no.

"At least I'm locked up in here with a beautiful girl and not some guy," he said.

* * *

Around midnight, Tammi told McAninch she was feeling sick. He let her go to the sink to throw up. Then he became concerned. "Are you all right? Can I get you some milk to settle your stomach?"

"Yes," Tammi said.

He went into the store and brought her some. Then he started to pace. A few minutes later, he went to the sink and began to vomit himself. When he returned, Tammi saw panic in his eyes.

"Are you scared?" she asked.

He didn't answer. But overhead they heard helicopters. Tammi pleaded again with McAninch to let her go. She was tired. She was sick.

"You're becoming a not-so-cool hostage," he told her.

* * *

At around 2 a.m., McAninch gathered flattened cardboard boxes and put them on the floor. Then he found some Bigfoot employee uniform shirts in the back room and laid them on the cardboard to make a bed. As he stretched out, blocking the front doorway, gun in hand, he asked Tammi, "You want to do something?"

"What!" Tammi said, surprised and angry. McAninch lay there looking at her as the minutes ticked by, then said, "Okay, I'm not even going to go there."

Tammi watched as he closed his eyes. All right, she thought. What if he goes to sleep? Should I run for it? In the end she decided not to. The doors were locked, and he still held the gun. And as far as she could tell, he never did drift off to sleep.

The negotiator called again, offering a cell phone to McAninch because the landline had become staticky. Send Tammi out for it; they'd leave it outside.

"I'm not sending her out there till you guys back off," McAninch said.

Taking a chance, Tammi walked to the front door, took the handle and pulled. "The door's locked," she yelled to the police.

"Get back here," McAninch ordered.

"Let me go get that phone. I'll come back," she pleaded.

After more negotiation with her and the police, McAninch finally agreed. But he wanted to make sure his "protection" would come back.

He began rummaging around in the store, searching. Suddenly he picked up a vacuum cleaner, grabbed a screwdriver and took it apart. He ripped the electrical cord free, and came for Tammi. He tied the cord around her waist.

Holding her on a tether, he let Tammi out the front door. In the interim, working in the shadows, the police had unlocked it. Tammi moved forward, looked, but couldn't find the phone. Enraged, McAninch yanked her in.

Back on the static-filled landline, the police explained that a new cell phone had been attached to a pole just outside the door. But McAninch was in no mood to listen.

*   *   *

As dawn broke, police demolition experts rigged the heavy back door with explosive charges. A SWAT team was ready to blow it open and rush the store.

At the same time, around 6:30 a.m., McAninch changed his mind and decided to send Tammi out once more to get the phone. He played her out on the cord. She opened the door, stepped forward, saw the phone on the ground and reached for it.

Policemen hidden in the shadows grabbed her by the arm and tried to pull her free. For a moment Tammi was trapped in a tug of war. But McAninch reeled her back in.

"Get back!" he yelled at the police. "Get back!" He fired a shot.

Police returned fire. One SWAT unit blew open the back door. Another unit rushed the front.

"Stop shooting! Stop shooting!" Tammi yelled. "I'm right here! I'm right here!" She fell to the floor and grabbed a plastic soda tray to shield her head.

Suddenly it was silent. The shooting stopped. She looked at McAninch, who was lying motionless across her leg—bullet wounds in his arm, leg and chest.

Tammi didn't scream or cry. She didn't know whether to run or not. She thought McAninch might still be able to shoot her. But he was dying. His mouth was open and there was a gaping hole under his chin pulsing out blood. He'd shot himself—he would never go back to prison.

The police moved to scoop her up, but she was still tethered to the bloody body. An officer cut the cord, and finally she was free.

*   *   *

Outside it was raining. Her shoe had come off. Held between two policemen, Tammi hopped on one foot across the wet parking lot. They took her to the command trailer to recover and talk with negotiators. Amazingly, her only injury was to her morning manicure—a broken nail.

Her husband, Shawn, ran to the trailer to meet her. They hugged, unable to speak, and Shawn began to cry. But Tammi was too burned out for tears.

She didn't cry that day or night or the next day. It wasn't until around midnight of the second day that she began to weep uncontrollably.

From the time she was a child, Tammi Smith had nightmares that someone was lurking in the dark waiting to kill her with a knife or a gun. After Bigfoot, she doesn't have that dream anymore.

KILLER ON CALL

by Max Alexander

Helen Dean was one of those lucky people who had managed to grow old gracefully. At 91 she was still active in the Eastern Star order, a sister group to the Masons. She was alert, quick to laugh, and looked much younger than her years. "She didn't have a lot of wrinkles," says her niece Sharon Jones.

In late August 1993, she was enjoying a smooth recovery from colon surgery at Warren Hospital in Phillipsburg, New Jersey, when a thin, sharp-featured male nurse entered her room. The nurse told Helen's son Larry to leave; when he finished his work and Larry returned a few minutes later, Helen angrily announced, "He stuck me!"

Larry thought that was odd, as his mother wasn't scheduled to receive any medications. Strange, too, was the location of the shot—on her inner thigh, where it was very hard to see. Just to be certain, Larry whipped out his Swiss Army knife and trained the magnifying glass on the spot. Sure enough, there was a tiny puncture wound in the skin. Later that day, the same nurse came in to clear dishes. "That's the man who stuck me!" Helen said again. Larry told his mother's doctors and other nurses, but beyond questioning some hospital staffers, they did nothing.

The next day, Helen began vomiting inexplicably, delaying

by several hours her discharge to a nursing home, where she was to receive physical therapy before going home. It came as a tremendous shock to her relatives when she died of heart failure that afternoon.

That night, Helen's son called the local prosecutor and told him that she'd been murdered. He had a suspect in mind. It was the male nurse who gave Helen the mysterious injection, and he knew his name—Charles Cullen.

* * *

Sharon Jones had remembered the nurse's name because Helen Dean's middle name happened to be Cullen. But not much else about Charlie Cullen stood out. An emotionally withdrawn man who could barely bring himself to converse with his own wife, Cullen had hidden in plain sight for years—blending in and getting by, despite a history of bizarre behavior.

Cullen was born in 1960 in West Orange, New Jersey, a densely populated blue-collar enclave of double-decker houses and winding streets. He was the youngest of eight kids—five of them girls—in a tight-knit Roman Catholic household that included his parents—Florence and bus driver Edmond—and an aunt who was a social worker. There might have been more children, but when Charlie was almost seven months old, his father died of an undisclosed illness, at age 56.

Growing up without a father in a large family consisting mainly of women, Charlie developed into an awkward kid who kept to himself. When neighbors can place him, they vaguely recall a boy who didn't have much to say. Robert Hull remembered that Cullen seldom responded with anything more than a perfunctory "fine" when asked how he was doing. In fact, things weren't so fine. When Charlie was 17, his mother was killed in a car accident.

Exactly how Cullen handled the loss of his second parent is unclear—but soon afterward he joined the Navy, serving as a technician for ballistic missiles on the *Woodrow Wilson*, a nuclear submarine.

It would be hard to imagine a less hospitable place for a recently orphaned, introverted teenager. Submarine duty is one of the most intense experiences in the military—dangerous even in peacetime—with men living together in close quarters for months. Some subs make frequent port calls, but not the *Wilson*; its mission was to remain undetected, cruising through ocean waters without breaking the surface for nine or ten weeks at a stretch. And while a sub's exact location might be a military secret, there are few secrets on a sub itself. Sailors' smallest character flaws are quickly exposed, and in an environment where a tiny mistake can turn into a fatal error, weakness is not tolerated.

All new sub recruits endure a period of "hazing," but shipmates say Petty Officer Second Class Charles Cullen was singled out for his flinching, geeky demeanor. "Charlie was one of those people everyone picked on," says Marlin Emswiler, his bunkmate. A frequent subject of gibes was Cullen's pasty skin tone. Petty Officer First Class Michael Leinen recalls the time Cullen severely sunburned his feet at the beach while the crew was on shore leave. "He refused to go to sick bay to have [the burn] treated because he thought he would get into trouble," says Leinen. "I had to force him to go."

Still, Emswiler says Cullen was basically a nice guy who enjoyed relaxing at weekend oyster roasts. "Charlie would give you the shirt off his back," he says. He was particularly helpful to the ship's doctor, according to Emswiler, who remembers Cullen volunteering to give vaccinations when sailors lined up for shore leave.

But Cullen's interest in medicine took a bizarre turn one day when Leinen found Cullen manning the missile controls while wearing a surgical gown, mask and gloves. At the time, Leinen thought Cullen was just trying to be funny, but he reported the bizarre incident to his superiors anyway. Years later, Leinen, who went on to work as a facilitator with mentally ill patients at a veteran's hospital, came to believe Cullen had been deeply troubled. "He didn't have a grasp on reality," he says. Eventually, Cullen was transferred out of sub duty, but his problems continued. Leinen heard Cullen attempted suicide a few years later, which may have led to his discharge in 1984. (Citing privacy rules, Navy officials will not confirm a suicide attempt.)

After his release, Cullen enrolled in the Mountainside Hospital School of Nursing, located just a few miles from where he grew up. He graduated in May 1987—two months after his brother James died suddenly at age 31, possibly from a drug overdose. A week later, Cullen married Adrienne Taub, a computer programmer, who has refused to speak to the press about her former husband. Shortly thereafter, Charles Cullen, RN, landed his first nursing job at Saint Barnabas Medical Center in Livingston, New Jersey.

Chief burn technician Jeanne Hackett worked with Cullen in a Saint Barnabas unit for severely burned patients. "His job was to make sure they were comfortable during their bandage change," she says. "It's the hardest time for the patients, and Charlie seemed very appropriate. He didn't have the warm, coddling part in him, but there weren't too many guys who did."

Hackett remembers Cullen as having a dry sense of humor. "You knew anything that came out of his mouth would get a chuckle," she says. She also describes him as a "nonstop worker" who was extremely intense. "He was a big coffee drinker and rarely paused for anything to eat," says Hackett. "One day I said, 'Charlie, I've never seen you sit down and have lunch. You can't keep going like this; you've got to take some time.' He said, 'No, I'm okay. I ate this morning, and I'll eat when I go home.'"

Home was a subject that rarely came up, says Hackett. "He never talked about his family life. I worked with him for a while before I found out that he had a wife and children." (Charlie and Adrienne's two daughters are now 16 and 12.) The male nurse certainly never shared his problems—including the breakup of his marriage.

* * *

In divorce papers filed in January 1993, Adrienne Cullen described a dysfunctional relationship in which her sullen, remote husband slept on the couch for three years and never took her out. Instead he immersed himself in his work. "He consistently works 12 to 36 hours of overtime each week," she wrote. "When I approach him about working less overtime, he implies that I am being unreasonable and selfish."

Adrienne described a 1991 trip they took to Disney World with her parents: "I was seven months pregnant. Charles never assisted me in disembarking buses or expressed any concern or compassion for the fact that I was very pregnant and on my feet all day. One night we went to a 'Wild West Show.' Charlie wandered off by himself, embarrassing me in front of my parents. When the show began, Charles began to drink beer." (The subsequent divorce order called for Cullen to "continue his current individual and alcohol counseling programs.")

At home, Adrienne claimed that her husband repeatedly

turned the heat off in winter—and when she complained, he retaliated by cranking the thermostat to 80. While his wife and daughters roasted in their bedrooms, "He sleeps in the living room with the window open," Adrienne charged.

Cullen apparently reserved much of his anger for the family's two Yorkshire terriers. "I was awakened many nights by the screams of these dogs," Adrienne said. Cullen once zipped a misbehaving pup into a bowling bag.

He was also losing it on the road, racking up tickets and fender benders left and right. In 1989 he was pulled over for speeding. In 1990 he ran a stop sign in Phillipsburg and caused a minor accident. Less than five months later, he ran another stop sign. By the time of his arrest, his driving record showed three accidents and three speeding tickets.

The ride was getting bumpy at work too. The nursing agency through which Cullen was then working at Saint Barnabas fired him in January 1992 for undisclosed reasons, and a month later he was hired at Warren Hospital in Phillipsburg. There, shortly after Adrienne filed for divorce, Cullen became obsessed with a nurse named Michelle Tomlinson, buying her an engagement ring after just one dinner date. One morning, soon after Tomlinson got back together with her old boyfriend, she woke up to find the glass smashed out of her back door and evidence that someone had entered her Palmer Township, Pennsylvania, home during the night. Later that morning, Cullen called and admitted to the break-in.

"I wanted to check on you," he told Tomlinson. "You know, to make sure you were okay, that you did not try anything—like suicide." Tomlinson was so shaken that she pressed charges.

When police called Cullen, says Palmer Township Police Chief Bruce Fretz, "he came right in and admitted to everything." After being fingerprinted, photographed and arraigned,

Cullen left and attempted suicide—ending up a patient in the same intensive-care unit where he worked at Warren Hospital. He was later admitted to Greystone Park Psychiatric Hospital in Parsippany, New Jersey.

Less than five months later, Cullen pleaded guilty to misdemeanor trespassing in the Tomlinson incident and was sentenced to a year's probation. At his plea hearing, Cullen said, "I have never in my life intentionally tried to inflict any distress or harm on anyone." Days later he appealed, representing himself and filing pages of handwritten motions detailing his assertion that he had not been stalking Tomlinson. "Their [sic] was a sexual, intamate [sic] relationship between Michelle Tomlinson and myself," he scrawled on one document to the court. Court and police papers show that Warren Hospital officials were well aware of Cullen's arrest and suicide attempt. Yet two months after breaking into Tomlinson's home and while still undergoing treatment for depression, he was back working long hours.

Cullen definitely needed the money: In his pretrial application for a public defender, he listed monthly expenses of $1,460 for child support, $300 for psychiatric treatment and $346 in minimum-balance credit card payments. (In 1998 he filed for bankruptcy.) But his enthusiasm for work apparently went beyond compensation. Exactly three weeks after his conviction, Cullen walked into Helen Dean's hospital room and asked her son to leave.

An autopsy on Dean was inconclusive, but because no injection had been ordered by a doctor, the hospital made Cullen take a lie detector test. He passed—then quit his job. The matter was dropped.

*   *   *

Cullen next stepped onto a merry-go-round of short-term positions, working at eight more hospitals or nursing homes in the next nine and a half years. He favored the hard-to-fill night shift, a time when nurses are less supervised. Meanwhile, his private life continued to spiral. In 1997, during a brief period when he was unemployed after being fired for poor performance from Morristown Hospital in New Jersey, Cullen was back as a patient in Warren's emergency room, being treated for a depression-related illness that may have been another suicide attempt.

He was working the night shift at the Liberty Nursing and Rehabilitation Center in Allentown, Pennsylvania, on May 7, 1998, when an elderly patient received an unauthorized dosage of insulin and eventually died. The man, Francis Henry, had been in a car accident and appeared to be in severe pain— barely able to mouth "I love you" to his wife. The nurse in charge of Henry, Kimberly Pepe, was fired over the incident.

Pepe claimed that the nursing home should have instead suspected Cullen, who had a patient in the same room and was already being monitored by the pharmacy for stealing drugs, including morphine and digoxin, a medication that is used to regulate the heart and can cause cardiac arrest if administered improperly. The nursing home denies Cullen was under investigation at the time, but Liberty eventually did fire him in late 1998 for failing to follow guidelines on medication delivery. Less than a week later, Cullen landed a job at Easton Hospital in Easton, Pennsylvania.

*   *   *

Kristina Toth had a bad feeling about the gaunt-looking male nurse who wheeled her 78-year-old father, Ottomar Schramm, out of Easton's emergency room. "I thought he was real cold,"

Toth recalls. "He didn't show any emotion." In his hand was a hypodermic needle. "What's that for?" Toth asked.

"In case his heart stops," replied the nurse.

Schramm's heart did indeed stop three days later, the last day of 1998. An autopsy revealed a digoxin overdose. Schramm, a retired steelworker, had been admitted after experiencing seizures; there was no medical reason for the digoxin in his system. Although the pathologist concluded the death was accidental, Toth suspected otherwise. By then Cullen was living in a basement apartment on a tidy block in Phillipsburg. "He kept to himself," says Charles Cook, who lived two doors down. "He was a nice neighbor; in the summer he kept his yard beautiful. On weekends sometimes his kids would visit."

But there were no children around on the morning of January 3, 2000. Upstairs neighbor Karen Ziemba woke to the smell of a strong fuel odor coming from the basement. When Cullen didn't come to the door, she called the police. Officer Bernie Kelly arrived, forced his way in and found a charcoal hibachi grill burning in the bathtub. Cullen had removed batteries from smoke detectors and blocked heat vents with insulation. "He wouldn't admit it was a suicide attempt," says Kelly. "He said he was trying to stay warm. I said, 'Charlie, you're a nurse. You know and I know what's going on here.'"

If only his employers had known. But privacy concerns kept his personal medical history out of sight.

A few months after the basement suicide attempt, Cullen landed his eighth nursing job, this one at St. Luke's Hospital in Bethlehem, Pennsylvania. He worked there two years but quit abruptly in June of 2002, after he was questioned about a stash of unopened heart medication found in a needle-disposal bin. Concerns over the number of deaths on his shift prompted a police investigation, but a forensic pathologist and an investigator from the state's nursing board could find no concrete evidence.

Next Cullen moved on to a hospital in nearby Allentown, where he was considered so odd that he was "weeded out" after 18 days, according to a hospital representative. By now he had been fired from four institutions, often under a cloud of suspicion over medication errors and unusual patient deaths. Relatives of victims, like Helen Dean's niece Sharon Jones, can't understand why investigators failed to pin any crimes on Cullen. "We know who did it, when he did it, and how," says Jones, adding that catching Cullen back in 1993 would have saved many lives.

Instead, Cullen kept working—and killing. After the Liberty Nursing Center fired him, personnel there notified the state Department of Health about the medication error. But no one bothered to call the police. Nor was the nursing home required to pass along its concerns to other hospitals who called for job references. Hospitals today (like other businesses) risk being sued if they make negative comments about former employees. As a result, even when a hospital grew alarmed enough to notify authorities, Cullen's misdeeds were not passed along to subsequent employers. No one was getting the big picture.

That picture was becoming increasingly grim in September 2002 when Cullen started work at Somerset Medical Center in Somerville, New Jersey. It was his tenth and last job.

Health care technology had changed considerably since Cullen first donned a nurse's uniform. At Somerset, the hospital used a high-tech computerized care system called Cerner that allowed health workers to punch up a patient's medical and drug history at a terminal within seconds. Another computer system, Pyxis, tracked drug disbursements. Pyxis worked like a cash register: By typing in data that included a patient's name and a nurse's ID number, a drawer for a particular drug would slide open.

Working the night shift as usual, Cullen became adept at circumventing the system to withdraw unauthorized drugs. Sometime during the evening of June 15, 2003, he ordered digoxin for one of his patients who had not been prescribed it. After picking up the drug, he tried to cover his tracks by canceling the order on the Pyxis computer. Meanwhile, he went into the Cerner system and accessed the records of Jin Kyung Han, a cancer patient who was not under his care.

The next morning, Han went into cardiac malfunction and was found to have high levels of digoxin in her system. She recovered after an antidote was administered, but died three months later.

Then, during the night of June 27, Cullen played his deadly game again—withdrawing digoxin for one of his own patients, canceling the order, and accessing the medical records of a heart-disease patient who was not his own. That patient, a Roman Catholic priest named Florian Gall, died the next morning. His body contained lethal amounts of digoxin.

At that point hospital officials could hardly ignore the situation. They alerted the New Jersey poison control center, but allowed Cullen to keep working while investigating other possibilities, including whether Han's condition could have been caused by an herbal tea she drank. Before long, Dr. Steven Marcus of poison control became convinced that someone was deliberately poisoning patients and notified the state health department.

Health officials began an investigation, but still Cullen kept working. On August 27, a patient in his ward received a nonfatal overdose of insulin, yet the hospital never reported the incident. (Somerset was later fined for that failure.) When another patient died after a suspicious drop in blood-sugar levels that could only have been caused by an insulin overdose, the hospital finally called the county prosecutor's office.

* * *

Belatedly, the hospital fired Cullen—on October 31, after discovering he had falsified employment history on his job application. The prosecutor's office, meanwhile, kept up its investigation. "The hospital's computer system made it pretty easy to track him," says Somerset County prosecutor Wayne J. Forrest. "We caught him red-handed by his ID number." On December 12 they arrested Cullen as he drove away from a Somerville restaurant.

When the police pulled him over, Cullen went quietly. As he had 10 years earlier when accused of the Pennsylvania break-in, he readily admitted to his crimes. Although initially charged on just two counts—murdering Reverend Gall and attempting to kill Han—Cullen said he had killed as many as 40 patients during the course of his career. If true, that would make him one of the worst serial killers in U.S. history.

And one of the most enigmatic. According to Forrest, Cullen claimed that the overdoses were mercy killings. But many of his victims were not mortally ill—or even in pain. Beatrice Yorker, director of the School of Nursing at San Francisco State University and an expert on killer nurses, says such a motivation is rarely an honest one. "These people are sociopaths mostly interested in getting their own needs met," she says. "I liken them to firefighters who set fires. Often what they need is power and control or excitement and attention." Unfortunately for Cullen's victims, it took years for the people around him to pay that attention. "I ask myself, What was I missing?" says Jeanne Hackett, Cullen's former colleague. "I can't imagine where that evil could be inside someone I knew and cared about."

We may never know what made Cullen a killer. As investigators in seven counties huddled to sort through the Cullen case, relatives of possible victims wondered what to do next. Several lawsuits against hospitals have been filed, and bodies long buried are being exhumed. In April 2004, New Jersey Governor James McGreevey signed a law that requires health care facilities to report all serious medical errors to the state. But Cullen's mobility across state lines suggests the need for stronger federal monitoring as well.

*   *   *

In April 2004, Cullen pleaded guilty to killing 13 patients and attempting to kill two others in Somerset County. He also confessed to the murder of Ottomar Schramm, and charges for his crimes are still pending in other counties. In return for his plea and for agreeing to cooperate with authorities, Cullen will be spared the death penalty and will instead spend the rest of his life in prison.

Among Cullen's confessions was the 1993 murder of Helen Dean. Sharon Jones attended the plea hearing and sat less than four feet from the man who murdered her aunt. "He remembered right down to the time of day and the dosage he used," she says. One thing Cullen didn't do was make eye contact. "As he passed by in front of us, he had his head hanging down, cocked a little bit to one side," Jones remembers. "He took a quick look and then turned his head back again. He looked completely blank of emotion."

Jones says that while getting justice brings some satisfaction, it does little to take away the pain she still feels. "My aunt was like a second mother to me, and someone other than

God made the decision that she should no longer be on this earth. Why did he pick her? That's the thing you always wonder." For Helen Dean and perhaps as many as 39 others, their loved ones can only hope that someday Charles Cullen will tell them why.

Charles Cullen is currently serving a life sentence and is incarcerated at New Jersey State Prison in Trenton.

HEIST

by Simon Worrall

It's Christmastime in Stockholm. December 22, 2000, 4:45 p.m., to be exact. Snow blankets the ground. The last visitors to the Nationalmuseum are putting on their coats, ready to leave. They're talking and laughing, but the festive mood is about to come to an end. Because just at that moment, thieves are parking a Mazda and a Ford sideways across the only two roads leading to the museum, a Renaissance-style palazzo at the tip of a peninsula, almost completely encircled by water. They douse the vehicles with barbecue lighter fluid and set them on fire. Then they strew steel spikes over the road to puncture the tires of any police cars that try to get through.

As the cars burst into flames, three members of the gang race into the museum. They wear ski masks and carry pistols and machine guns. "Everybody lie down!" shouts the gang leader, putting a pistol to the head of a guard.

Screams echo through the marble halls as two gang members sprint up the stairs. They know exactly where to go, having studied floor plans for months. Their job is made easier by the fact that there are no glass screens or cameras. Using bolt cutters, they quickly pluck a Rembrandt from the wall and stuff it into a bag. Then they cut the wires securing two

Renoirs and race back down the stairs with their booty, past a woman who lies whimpering on the floor.

The gang leader pulls his pistol away from the head of the terrified guard and jams it into his denim jacket. Then the three masked men rush out of the building. They turn left, and left again, then sprint along the wharf behind the museum, where an associate is waiting for them in a speedboat.

The boat heads east, past Skeppsholm Island, under Danvikstull Bridge, and across a bay. At a harbor used by fishermen, the thieves tie up the boat and leap ashore, where they disappear. In less than half an hour, the most daring art theft of the century is over.

* * *

Sweden is in mourning. Losing the Renoirs was a shock, but the Rembrandt has been a national treasure since its arrival in 1956. To get it back, the Swedes ultimately look to the world's foremost art detective. A self-avowed keeper of the world's cultural flame, Robert Wittman is at the time the head of the FBI's Art Crime Team—a specialist force of 13 agents dedicated to hunting down stolen art (he left recently to work for a law firm that specializes in stolen and fraudulent art). In a career stretching back 20 years, he has helped recover more than $250 million in artwork, including paintings by Norman Rockwell and Mark Rothko, gold body armor taken from a tomb in Peru, and Geronimo's warbonnet.

"Saving these things brings us closer together as human beings," says Wittman, explaining why he goes to work every day. Besides, Rembrandt's *Self Portrait* will look good on the résumé.

No artist painted himself as obsessively as Rembrandt van

Rijn. In more than 90 self-portraits—from the tousle-haired youth of the 1620s to the hoary old man of 1669, the year of his death—he created a record of human aging without equal in Western art. *Self Portrait*, from 1630, is one of only five paintings he executed on copper, and one of his smallest, the size of a hardback book. But packed into this space is a work of staggering genius: a portrait of the Dutch artist as a young man, age 24, that has all the energy and pathos of a living person.

Dressed in a dark-brown coat, with a black beret pushed insouciantly off his frizzy chestnut hair, Rembrandt stares out at us with an expression that is both vulnerable and steely. A costly gold leaf overlay makes the colors glow, as though lit from within. When it was first sold in Rotterdam in the 17th century, it changed hands for 35 florins, the equivalent of $35. Today you would need $40 million to own it.

Which goes a long way toward explaining why art theft is a growth industry. It's estimated that the worldwide trade in stolen and forged art is worth upwards of $6 billion annually. Only drug dealing, gunrunning, and money laundering are more profitable. Some museums will pay a ransom to get the artwork back. Others aren't given that option by the thieves, says Wittman. In some cases, the robbers try to sell the work on the open market. But this rarely works—after all, a knowledgeable collector isn't going to buy a stolen Monet that he can't display publicly. So the purloined artwork tends to stay in the underworld for an average of seven years before a buyer is sought. If it's sold, it's usually for about 7 to 10 percent of its legitimate value. Not bad, considering some are worth millions.

The Swedish authorities don't have to wait long to recover

one of the Renoirs, *La Conversation*. Acting on a tip, police rescue the painting. Thirteen people are arrested, among them three Iraqi-born brothers. Two of them, Baha and Dieya Kadhum, are acquitted; only the middle brother, Safa, is convicted. Still, the other two works of art are nowhere to be found. And after Baha and Dieya walk free, the trail goes cold.

*   *   *

Los Angeles. March 25, 2005, 3 p.m. Officers from the local organized-crime squad arrest a suspected member of a Eurasian crime syndicate while looking for drugs.

They don't find any dope this time. Instead they find a painting, a portrait of a woman with a soft bow at her neck. To find out who she is, they call on a local curator, as well as Bob Wittman and his FBI Art Crime Team. After photographs are scanned and databases checked, the painting is identified as the other Renoir, *Jeune Parisienne*, stolen nearly five years ago in Sweden.

When task force agents interrogate one of the thieves nabbed with the Renoir, he tells them the whereabouts of the other, far more valuable painting snatched from the Nationalmuseum: the Rembrandt. He also reveals the names and contact information of the people holding *Self Portrait*.

With phone numbers in hand, Wittman and his Swedish counterpart, Detective Magnus Osvald of the Stockholm police, concoct a sting operation to bring the Rembrandt back.

"I played an undercover art expert for a European organized crime group in America," Wittman explains. "I flew to Copenhagen, then got into contact with the people in Stockholm who were holding the painting."

*   *   *

The Scandic hotel, Copenhagen. September 15, 2005, 10 a.m. Wittman waits in his room for a phone call. He is used to living out of suitcases. Some months, he spends more time on his cell phone than he does at home with his three kids and wife of 23 years. Besides the United States, he has worked in Brazil, Ecuador, France—18 countries in total. There are times when he wakes up and can't remember what city he's in.

Today, as usual, he has checked into a hotel under a false name, using false travel documents. Pretending to be someone else is a big part of his job. It helps that he has one of those faces that are easy to forget. No distinguishing features, no scars, no cauliflower ears. Average height, average build. A regular-looking guy. Put him in a crowded room and he would blend into the background, like a camouflaged moth on a tree trunk.

Sometimes that can be a problem. Three years ago, in a Madrid hotel, he had to throw himself on the floor as a Spanish SWAT team burst into the room to arrest Angel Suarez Flores, the head of a crime syndicate. Flores had offered Wittman one of the gems of medieval Flemish art, *The Temptation of Saint Anthony,* by Pieter Bruegel the Elder. It had been stolen from the penthouse of Spain's richest woman, along with paintings by Goya, Pissarro, and Japanese painter Foujita—a $50 million haul. When the cops tore into the room, Wittman was worried they wouldn't know he was on their side. He got out alive by diving behind a bed, shouting, "Don't shoot! *Bueno hombre!* Good guy!"

*   *   *

As Wittman checks the money he has brought from the States to buy the Rembrandt, $250,000 in cash, his cell phone rings. It's the Swedish police, who have been doing surveillance all the way from Stockholm. "The three art thieves came by train, with one of them holding the painting in a shopping bag," he recalls. "They switched trains at the Danish-Swedish border."

The Swedish police do not arrest the men right away. They want to catch them selling Wittman the stolen Rembrandt. Baha and Dieya Kadhum, the two acquitted Iraqi-born brothers, plus a 29-year-old Swede named Alexander Lindgren, think they are about to pull off the final move in one of the biggest art heists in history. Instead they are walking into a perfectly laid trap.

In Copenhagen, Lindgren and the two Kadhum brothers walk around the hotel a couple of times to make sure they are not being followed. Wittman, using the phone number he got from the snitch in L.A., calls them on their cell phone and arranges to meet Baha Kadhum, the leader, in the lobby.

Kadhum is in his late 20s: black hair, lean face, sallow skin, hooded eyes. He is wearing designer jeans, a T-shirt, and expensive leather shoes. "We discussed how we would do the trade," says Wittman. "We would go upstairs. I would flash the money. If he's happy with that, I'll see the painting, which is outside with the two other guys."

At the heart of Wittman's job is what he calls "befriending and betraying." In every undercover operation, there is a tipping point, a moment when the bad guys move from suspicion to trust. Wittman calls this "the moment of acceptance." The period just before that is the most dangerous. A sweaty lip, an overeager smile, and he could blow his cover and end up dead. But years of practicing the art of deception ensure that, as Kadhum walks into the hotel room, Wittman looks as affable as a high school history teacher. It's Kadhum who's jumpy, while Wittman pats him down to make sure he isn't carrying a gun or a knife. "He keeps fidgeting," recalls Wittman. Kadhum's eyes dart around as though he thinks someone else is there. "Only when he has the money in his hands does he begin to relax. He trusts the money. And that is his big mistake."

*   *   *

Kadhum says he will return with the painting in a few minutes. A half hour later and no Kadhum. What if something has gone wrong? What if Wittman's cover has been blown? What if he isn't clean?

Keeping clean is FBI-speak for making sure an agent has not been tailed. Art thieves are a cautious lot, says Wittman, which means "I usually have people following me for a while. So you don't go anywhere you shouldn't until you have been cleaned. But you always have to be aware of that possibility."

And you always practice countersurveillance. You watch the people watching you. But never alone. Wittman is always part of a team. The team is his shield, his radar. This time, the Swedish and Danish police have set up operations in a room a floor above him, as well as in the room next door. Wittman's room is wired, and there's a miniature camera hidden in a lamp.

"After I flash him the money, Kadhum leaves the hotel room and goes downstairs," says Wittman. "The other two guys are on the street with the bag. But the three of them then go to another hotel room where a fourth guy *actually* has the painting." He smiles. "They are good. The other bag is just a dummy."

When Kadhum finally does come back to the hotel, he's carrying the painting in a red felt bag tied tightly with cord. "I had a hard time opening the bag," recalls Wittman with a laugh, "what with there being no knives in the room!"

But untie it he did. And there it was, the Rembrandt.

"You ever take it out of the frame?" asks Wittman.

"I never touched it," says Kadhum.

"You an art lover?"

"No. I am just in it for the money."

Wittman takes the painting into the bathroom and uses a miniature ultraviolet lamp and a black light to check it for signs of forgery or damage. The end is only seconds away now, and soon all hell will break loose.

Turning off the lamp, he gives the prearranged signal. "It's a done deal!" he says to Kadhum in a loud voice.

As the door flies open and Danish police barrel in, Wittman shields the painting with his body. The five agents are encased in body armor and are toting semiautomatic weapons. "Freeze!" they scream at Kadhum.

*   *   *

Nationalmuseum, Stockholm. September 20, 2005, 6 p.m. Champagne corks pop and cameras flash as Rembrandt's *Self Portrait* is rehung. For the people of Sweden, the painting is a dear friend. Bulletproof glass and security cameras help ensure it never leaves them again.

There is no bubbly for Wittman. He is already back in America, undercover, working another case. The guests toasting the return of their beloved Rembrandt have no idea how complicated the sting operation was. Or how a quiet American with a face no one remembers risked his life to help recover it.

But Wittman's no martyr. Just ask him what it's like to hold a Rembrandt.

"It's a eureka moment," he says, grinning widely. "It's always a eureka moment."

The Kadhum brothers and Alexander Lindgren were convicted of receiving stolen goods, but their sentences were later overturned by a Swedish appeals court, which ruled they were "provoked" by American and Swedish police. They are still living in Sweden.

THE ALMOST-PERFECT MURDER

by Robert F. Howe

Donnah Winger couldn't have been in brighter spirits. The 31-year-old operating room technician was with her husband, Mark, at his Illinois Department of Nuclear Safety office to show off three-month-old Bailey, the little girl they were in the process of adopting. Mark's coworkers fussed over the baby and remarked how the popular couple now truly seemed complete. "She always wanted a family," says Donnah's stepfather, Ira Drescher, who notes that a medical condition had prevented her from having biological offspring. "This was something she had dreamt about."

Later that afternoon, shortly after the proud parents had returned to their modest brick home on Westview Drive in Springfield, Mark headed to the basement for a workout. He was jogging on his treadmill when he heard a loud thump upstairs. Alarmed, he bolted up the basement steps and, hearing his baby's cry, turned right through the bathroom and into the bedroom. Finding Bailey wailing and alone on the bed, Winger snatched up the .45 semiautomatic he had hidden in his nightstand and sped toward the dining room.

There, he witnessed a stranger kneeling over his wife, wielding fierce blows with a claw hammer. The assailant paused to glance up at Winger, and then raised the hammer to strike again. Winger took quick aim and shot him twice in the head. Frantic, he then phoned 911.

When police arrived, they found Winger bent over Donnah, who lay facedown in an inky pool of blood. An officer, who had his own camera in his car, snapped three quick images of the crime scene as medics attended to Donnah and her attacker, who both still had feeble pulses. Police then led Winger into his bedroom, where, his voice quaking, he detailed what he'd seen. When an officer informed him that a driver's license identified the intruder as Roger Harrington, Winger burst out, "That's the man!"

He explained how Donnah had met Harrington when she returned with Bailey the previous Wednesday, August 23, from a visit to her parents' house in Florida. She had booked a van to get her home from the St. Louis airport. Harrington, 27, was at the wheel. He had terrified her by speeding down the highway, describing how a menacing spirit named Dahm sometimes urged him to hurt people, and boasting about orgies staged at his trailer in rural Sangamon County.

Winger said that he was at a business conference in Chattanooga, Tennessee, when Donnah called and described her harrowing ride. He instructed her to write down what had happened, and then phoned Harrington's employer to complain. A few days later, he also personally called the driver, then on suspension, to warn him to steer clear of his family.

As Winger was wrapping up his chilling recitation, Donnah and Harrington were rushed to the hospital, where they died within the hour. Meanwhile, investigators checked out Winger's story. On the refrigerator, they found Donnah's note about her frightening drive with Harrington. Running checks on him, they established that he was a divorced high school dropout who had previously been arrested for battery and had also had a brief stay in a mental health facility. They learned too that he'd told many people about his evil spirit Dahm—his name for a Halloween mask he kept in his trailer. Police were soon convinced the Wingers had fallen victim to a psychopath.

All the officers were in agreement, save one. Det. Doug Williamson, relatively new to homicide, was reluctant to contradict his more seasoned colleagues but was privately troubled. "Winger would turn on and off emotion rather easy, yet there were never any tears," recalls Williamson, now a sergeant with the Springfield Police. "That wasn't normal."

There was another thing. Winger claimed to have cradled Donnah's head as she lay on the dining room floor fighting off death. Yet Williamson says he noticed Winger had blood on the back of his right hand, but none on the palm. Plus it seemed strange that a loving husband would comfort his wife as she gasped for breath, and then lay her facedown, as she was found, on the gore-smeared carpet.

* * *

Outside the Winger home, Williamson had run a check on a brown 1988 Oldsmobile Delta parked conspicuously on the wrong side of the street. As he suspected, it was Harrington's. Inside the car, something caught his eye. On the front seat, he found a blank bank deposit slip. Written on the back was the Wingers' address, Mark Winger's name and, strangely, a time: 4:30, just about the time of the killings.

The day after the deaths, Winger met again with detectives, who were already wrapping up their investigation. They asked if there was anything unusual in the house, and Winger mentioned a mug and a pack of Marlboro 100s that had been left in the dining room. Detectives concluded the items belonged to Harrington, but Williamson found it peculiar that a killer would bring his smokes along.

Williamson said he wanted to chase down new leads, but his superiors were convinced that Harrington was the culprit. "They're great detectives—they really are," says Williamson, who didn't press his misgivings. "But for whatever reason, they misinterpreted the facts." The evidence, including all the bloodied clothes, the gun, Donnah's note, the deposit slip found in Harrington's car, and the photos, were all filed away. Case closed.

Winger's family and friends gathered to comfort the distraught husband. A graduate of the Virginia Military Institute and an Army veteran who had become an engineer, Winger expressed his appreciation in a letter to the local paper: "On behalf of Bailey and me, as well as Donnah's parents and siblings and mine, I want to publicly express our thank-you to the people in this community whose concern and understanding at this difficult time will long be remembered."

When the notice was published in October 1995, it seemed a gracious final gesture in a horrifying case. Yet there would be much more to come. Williamson couldn't shake his doubts, and eventually others came to sense that something was amiss.

*   *   *

For the first few nights after Donnah's death, Winger stayed at the home of Rabbi Michael Datz and his wife. They were friends who were expecting a baby and had a nursery that Bailey could use. Deann Schultz, one of Donnah's closest friends and a surgical nurse, also slept at the rabbi's that first night. "Deann stayed at our house presumably because she was a nurse and had kids, so she would know how to handle Bailey," recalls Rabbi Datz. But he adds, "We had no clue what was really going on."

Within a few months, Winger had hired nanny Rebecca Simic to care for Bailey. Simic and Winger soon became involved, marrying in October 1996 and moving to a farmhouse in nearby Pleasant Plains. Together, the couple would have three more children.

Winger kept in close touch with investigators over the following years. "Mark kept injecting himself," says Williamson. "He kept calling, and he'd say, 'Hey, I'm getting married,' or 'Hey, I'm coming in to get my gun back.'" He called often enough for Williamson's partner, Det. Charlie Cox, to grow suspicious, wondering if Winger wasn't double-checking to make sure detectives had really dropped the case. After that, Cox and Williamson rarely spent a free moment together without discussing the killings. "There are always cases that leave lingering questions," says Williamson. "But if we were having a beer or going on a fishing trip, this is the one we'd talk about."

*   *   *

In early 1999, police got their break: a call from an attorney saying Deann Schultz wanted to talk. Schultz had fallen into such despair since her friend's death that she'd attempted to take her life four times. Finally, her psychiatrist persuaded her to divulge her terrible secret. The story she told began a few weeks before the slayings. Shortly after confiding in Donnah that she was unhappy with her marriage and considering going back to a former boyfriend, Schultz received a call from Winger, who said he was attracted to her. In a matter of days, they began their affair at an Illinois hotel, and later got together in Winger's red pickup truck near a local playground.

Schultz stated that shortly after she began seeing Winger, he led her to believe that they would someday be together. In one of her most telling recollections, he had said, "It would be easier if Donnah died." And there was more. The Wingers had told Schultz and her husband about Donnah's wild ride with Harrington, so Deann said she knew exactly who Winger was referring to the day before the murders when he said, "I need to get that van driver in my house."

When she first came forward, Schultz spoke freely with police, but she later received immunity so her trial testimony could not be used against her. Det. Jim Graham, who spoke several times with Schultz, laments that despite all that Winger had said to her, "She didn't do anything to stop it."

Schultz had failed to prevent the crime, but her story was all police needed to reopen the case. Investigators' first step was to retrieve the bloodied clothing that had been taken as evidence at the time of the crime and send it off to a blood-stain pattern expert. The expert reported back that he found blood spatter from Donnah on Winger's clothing, but not on Harrington's. In addition, he observed the castoff of Donnah's blood on the dining room wall was inconsistent with Winger's description of the killing.

Police then scrutinized the crime-scene photos, which had been sealed away without ever having been looked at. They showed Harrington's body in a position completely different from what Winger had described.

Investigators reviewed the 911 tapes. Winger had placed the 911 call but hung up midway through it. "In the background, Harrington is moaning," says State's Attorney John Schmidt. "Then suddenly, Winger says, 'My baby's crying. I've got to go. I'll call you right back,' and click."

In light of the 911 tape, police placed new importance on an earlier statement made by Winger's neighbor that at 4:30 p.m., about the time Winger hung up on the call, she heard what she thought was a single gunshot. Winger insisted he fired two consecutive shots at Harrington, yet police now concluded that the shots were several minutes apart, the second one aimed to silence Harrington. In fact, blood patterns on the floor suggested that Winger rolled Harrington over onto his back before firing the second bullet into the man's forehead.

But perhaps the most persuasive bit of evidence had been in police possession from the start: the note found in Harrington's car. Winger claimed he called Harrington the morning of his wife's death to tell him to stay away from Donnah. But in new conversations with Harrington's friends, police learned, from three people who were at Harrington's trailer when the call came in, that he was summoned for a 4:30 meeting at the Winger residence—all of which Harrington wrote on a roommate's deposit slip.

It all dovetailed with an ominous call that Deann Schultz said she received early on the afternoon of the murder. It was Winger, and he asked, "Will you love me no matter what?"

Finally, prosecutors felt they had sufficient evidence to secure an indictment, and on August 23, 2001, officers took Mark Winger into custody. He was then held on $10 million bail.

During the trial, prosecutors painted an eerie picture of what they believed happened at the Wingers' home on the day of the murder. Harrington arrived as requested, unarmed, and set his mug and cigarettes down in the dining room before Winger ushered him into the kitchen, where the note Donnah had written hung on the refrigerator. Harrington may have bent over to read it, or perhaps was forced to his knees at gunpoint. Then Winger shot him once in the head. When Donnah, who had been playing with Bailey in the bedroom, burst in to see what had happened, Winger swung the hammer into her head. She collapsed facedown, and he struck her at least six more times, showering blood onto the adjacent wall.

Jurors in last spring's trial found the state's case persuasive. On June 5, 2002, Winger, now 40, was found guilty of two counts of murder. He is serving a sentence of life without parole and, still claiming innocence and insisting that he was set up by a jilted Deann Schultz, has appealed the conviction. (Bailey and his other three children reside with his wife Rebecca, who continues to stand by his side.)

One vital element in the case has yet to be solved to everyone's satisfaction: motive. Some observers believe it was the affair—that Winger feared Donnah would find out he was seeing Schultz, demand a divorce, and take away Bailey. Others think Winger was motivated by greed. After Donnah's death, he received about $200,000 in insurance and another $25,000 from the state's fund for crime victims. In the end, investigators suspect he was motivated by a combination of factors. One thing is certain, says Ira Drescher, "My family was destroyed for a long time after this. He betrayed us all."

Mark Winger appealed his conviction, but it was upheld. Winger then tried to hire a fellow prisoner to kill Deann Schultz and a friend who did not post $1 million bail for him. He was found guilty of solicitation to commit murder in 2007 and was sentenced to an additional 35 years in prison. Winger is now serving his sentences in Menard Correctional Center in Illinois and is ineligible for parole. Rebecca Simic divorced Winger when he went to prison and is raising their three children as well as Bailey.

THE KILLER AMONG US

by Max Alexander

The potato fields that roll up to the edge of New Sweden were still dusted with snow on Sunday, April 27, 2003. Even by the standards of northern Maine it had been a tough winter, and the old furnace in the parsonage of the Gustaf Adolph Evangelical Lutheran Church was giving up the ghost. The church council had gathered after services to decide who would install a new heater. Council member Dick Ruggles, a 64-year-old retired ironworker, grabbed a cup of coffee and headed into the meeting.

He lasted about five minutes. "I asked a question of one of the members," says Ruggles, "and before he could answer, I had to leave and go to the men's room." When the vomiting briefly let up, Ruggles staggered out to find his wife, who had been chatting over coffee in the kitchen with Erich Margeson. "Fran," he said, "I have to go home now!"

Home was a white clapboard farmhouse just up the road, but Fran had to stop the car twice for Dick. Once there, the violent nausea continued, and severe diarrhea added to Dick's woes. When Fran went into the bedroom to change out of her church clothes, she suddenly felt sick herself. "I didn't make it back to the bathroom," she says. "I just could not stop vomiting."

Sometime between three and four that afternoon, the phone rang. It was Erich Margeson's wife, Alana, calling to say she'd just taken Erich to the hospital. Erich, a 30-year-old potato farmer, was also violently ill. Soon came another call: Dale Anderson, who had been at church, was sick too. When Barb Bondeson called around five, Dick and Fran were too ill to speak. Barb called Fran's sister, Julie Adler, who had skipped church that day. She raced over with her son, who had to carry Dick to the car.

With a population that hovers just over 600, New Sweden has no hospital of its own. Fortunately, an emergency room is just eight miles away, in the town of Caribou. Staffers at the Cary Medical Center take pride in their high-tech, point-of-care service. But Cary's greatest asset is its close relationship with the community. Its doctors know their patients from the local cross-country ski trails, not the medical charts. With only 37 beds and a small staff of nurses, Cary is set up for car accidents and cardiac arrests—not outbreaks of violent illness.

Yet an outbreak is exactly what Cary had by Sunday evening, as a total of 12 church members showed up retching and gasping. Patty Carson, the hospital's infection control officer, remembers, "My first thought was, 'Some poor old lady who made the potato salad is gonna be so upset.'" Thinking fast, Carson alerted the state's Bureau of Health to a possible food poisoning in New Sweden. Then she grabbed a notepad and headed for the patient wards, looking for answers.

It didn't take long for Carson to change her mind about the cause of the outbreak. The patients had eaten a variety of food in the church kitchen—tuna sandwiches, sponge cake, banana bread with icing—most of it left over from a bake sale the day before. The only common denominator was the coffee; every patient had sipped a cup, and they all recalled it tasted funny— "bitter," "metallic" or just plain "bad." And all got sick within an hour of drinking the brew. As a microbiologist, Carson knew that food-borne organisms typically take several hours or more to cause illness. And she doubted that any dangerous bacteria could thrive in the hot, acidic environment of a coffee urn.

Dr. Daniel Harrigan, the ER physician on duty, was coming to the same conclusion. "These people had blood pressures that were much lower than you would expect from food poisoning," he says. The most critical patient was Reid Morrill, the church's head usher and a beloved local character known for his homemade ice cream and for once hitting a hole in one at the Caribou Country Club. Morrill, 78, was still recovering from cardiac bypass surgery earlier in the year. Dr. Harrigan golfed with Morrill; now his links partner was hooked up to a ventilator. Recalls Harrigan: "I told Patty that this has to be a poisoning of some sort, and to call the poison center."

Morrill was one of four patients, including Fran Ruggles, admitted to Cary that night. Margeson and four others felt well enough after a few hours to go home. Convinced they were not contagious (and facing a shortage of beds), the hospital released them. Three additional patients, Dick Ruggles among them, needed more serious care but were stable enough to be transferred to the closest acute-care facility, Eastern Maine Medical Center in Bangor, 170 miles south.

As the hospital in Bangor was preparing to receive the patients, another medical team was swinging into action at the Northern New England Poison Center in Portland, 300 miles downstate. The center's medical director, Dr. Anthony Tomassoni, had been studying the charts of all the New Sweden patients. It was a little after three o'clock Monday morning when he called Dr. Harrigan. "I'm thinking heavy metals," he said. The toxicologist thought some New Sweden patients were experiencing a condition known as acidosis, resulting from the body's inability to use oxygen effectively. That could be caused by lead or antimony (an element in batteries), but arsenic was at the top of his list. "At the same time," remembers Tomassoni, "we thought, jeez, arsenic in northern Maine, what are the chances?"

Plenty, it turned out. Arsenic was once commonly used in potato farming as a so-called topkiller. A week before the harvest, farmers would spray a dilution of inorganic arsenic on the plants' bushy green tops to kill them off—allowing the potato skins to toughen. Today farmers use less poisonous herbicides, but it would not be unusual to find jars of powdered arsenic in barns around potato country.

Shortly after Harrigan and Tomassoni got off the phone, Reid Morrill died. Louise Beaupre, wife of another victim, recalled that only a week before, Morrill, still ailing from heart surgery, had said, "I don't know if I'm ever gonna feel okay." She had responded, "Of course you will." The next Sunday, she says, "He was all pink cheeks, smiling and laughing. I said 'I think somebody's feeling better!' And he said 'Yep, I am.' And I can still see him standing there with a cup of coffee in his hand."

Morrill's death triggered the attention of the state medical examiner, as well as the national news media. The case was gaining urgency.

Arsenic can be identified only with specialized equipment. The nearest lab with that capability was the state's Health and Environmental Testing Laboratory in the capital of Augusta—230 miles south of Caribou. Early Monday morning, a state trooper left Cary Medical Center with the patients' fluid samples, his siren wailing down Interstate 95. Also in the back of his cruiser was the coffee urn from the Gustaf Adolph Lutheran Church.

The results came back at about eight o'clock Monday night: Inconceivably high levels of arsenic were found in all the patient samples, as well as the coffee. Dr. Tomassoni was too shocked to congratulate himself on his diagnosis. "I never thought I would see something like this in my career," he says. That's when the state police were notified.

Lieutenant Dennis Appleton of the Maine State Police Criminal Investigation Division is not the type to jump to conclusions. Rather than assume the worst, he hoped his investigation would uncover an innocent, albeit tragic, explanation. On Tuesday, Appleton had the church sealed off and a team of detectives on-site. The search was unsettling. "After several days of examining the church from basement to attic," Appleton recalls, "we found nothing that would have contributed to an accidental poisoning—no jar of arsenic in the cupboard that had been mistaken for the sugar bowl."

When Fran Ruggles heard she had been poisoned with arsenic, she assumed it was environmental: "We'd had a lot of rain and snow. I thought it must be in the water." Tomassoni knew otherwise, estimating the level of poison would have required "a fistful or two" of pure powdered arsenic dumped directly into the coffee urn. Detectives began interviewing patients—now victims—about possible motives. None of them had a clue. Recalls Fran, "I just could not accept the fact that this was done deliberately."

She wasn't alone. In a state famous for insular small towns, New Sweden is in a class by itself. The community was founded in 1870 by 50 Swedish homesteaders, lured across the sea by the promise of free land and a new life. New Sweden is still largely populated by descendants of those settlers; about half of the 16 arsenic victims are Swedish. With its Midsommar celebration and *fiskare frukosts* (fisherman's breakfasts), the town retains closer ties to Sweden than to mainstream America.

Even tighter than the community is the congregation at the Gustaf Adolph church, built on a hill overlooking New Sweden by the original settlers in 1880. The picturesque chapel, with its steeple rising above farm and forest, is the oldest active Lutheran church in Maine. To many, the idea that a member of the small congregation (46 people attended church that Sunday) had poisoned them was unthinkable. Fran Ruggles echoed the feeling of the group when she told detectives, "You're going to have to prove it to me."

Doctors at Cary Medical Center had little time to ponder motivation. Once arsenic was diagnosed, all the patients who were released the night before had to be called back for additional treatment. And as the day progressed, new patients started showing up—some who had sipped a tiny bit of coffee and not gotten sick (tests showed potentially fatal doses of arsenic in them as well), and others, like carpenter Lester Beaupre, 53, who initially thought he had the flu.

Beaupre, a Vietnam veteran who once spent nine weeks in the hospital with meningitis, wasn't about to go to the emergency room for a little stomach bug. He spent Sunday night at home, his wife, Louise (who has never tasted coffee in her life), keeping him hydrated with Gatorade. On Monday, says Louise, "when they called and told me about Reid's death, I said to Lester, 'Okay, this is it. Put your clothes on.'" On the way to the hospital, Lester remembers, the snowbanks looked purple. "That's when I knew this was serious," he recalls.

Arsenic travels rapidly to every organ in the body, where it slows the conversion of oxygen to energy. Without energy, the heart's electrical activity falters, lungs fill with fluid, kidneys fail, nerve tissue is damaged, and the brain starts to short-circuit. Arsenic can affect almost anything and everything in the anatomy, which is why symptoms can range from cardiac arrest to seeing purple snow.

The most effective proven antidote is a drug known as British anti-lewisite, or BAL. It attaches to the arsenic molecules, drawing them out of the bloodstream and into the urine. It's a nasty drug to administer; the only way to ingest BAL is by mixing it with peanut oil, then injecting the greasy solution directly into muscle tissue—an excruciating ordeal.

It's also expensive, costing hundreds of dollars per dose. The price, and the rarity of arsenic poisoning, explains why BAL is not lying around on hospital pharmacy shelves. But with foresight that now seems miraculous, in the wake of the 2001 terrorist attacks Dr. Tomassoni had persuaded Maine's Bureau of Health to purchase BAL doses for the state's largest hospitals.

As the victims endured painful treatment and round-the-clock fluid testing, more bad news came on Friday: Church member Daniel Bondeson, a 53-year-old bachelor potato farmer, nurse's aide and high school ski coach, fatally shot himself in the chest. In his farmhouse, where he was discovered by his brother Carl, was a note in which he implicated himself in the tragedy, according to police.

The victims were stunned. "Danny was a friend of ours," says Dick Ruggles. Lester Beaupre had gone to high school with Bondeson; he still describes him as "probably the nicest person you'll ever meet."

Bondeson, a former member of the church council, was a quiet man, but active in the community. Dr. Harrigan had run in races with him. Another victim, Ralph Ostlund, often skied with him. Says Erich Margeson, "Danny was always interested in helping people if they had a problem." Louise

Beaupre, who describes Bondeson as "pleasant but shy," says, "My feeling is he just snapped. There's no logical reason. It's beyond comprehension."

But why?

"We're all scratching our heads," Erich explains. Police have not released the text of Bondeson's suicide letter. But Alan Harding, an attorney representing Bondeson's estate, told local newspapers that in the note Bondeson said he wanted to give five church members a "bellyache" like they had given him. Harding also said the note indicated Bondeson did not know the poison was arsenic. Lieutenant Appleton won't comment on Harding's statements except to stress that the lawyer has not personally seen the letter. One theory is that Bondeson was angry because his family had given the church a communion table that wasn't being used. "There were some hurt feelings," says one church member. But arsenic? "It's hard to think about," says Erich Margeson.

As the community struggled to understand, police dropped another bomb: Bondeson, they said, without offering additional details, did not act alone. Church members say they have no idea why police would have come to this conclusion. Anyone could have entered the unlocked church kitchen during the Saturday bake sale or before Sunday service. When residents of New Sweden, many of whom didn't even own keys, were advised to start locking their doors, and a police guard was posted at the hospital, Alana Margeson says, "the air in the community was so heavy."

Months later, New Sweden hasn't lightened up much, and detectives are no closer to an arrest, although they say they have one or more suspects.

Meanwhile, doctors can only speculate on the survivors' long-term prognosis; elevated cancer risk is one scary possibility.

THE SPY'S SON

Left: Nathan Nicholson (left) with his father, Jim Nicholson, at the Federal Correctional Institution in Sheridan, Oregon, in 2003. Right: The notebook Nathan used to write down questions from the Russians for his father

THE DRIVE OF HIS LIFE

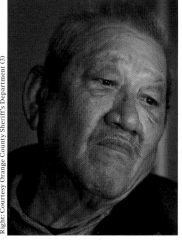

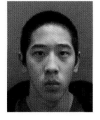

Long Ma (far left) was certain he was going to die when he was kidnapped by prison escapees (clockwise from top left) Bac Duong, Jonathan Tieu, and Hossein Nayeri.

THE INTRUDER

Suzanne Marotti and her boys (from left) Tommy, Daniel, and Matthew—safe at home again

I HUNTED DOWN THE WOMAN WHO STOLE MY LIFE

Karen Lodrick, victim of identity theft

Maria Nelson had six prior criminal convictions.

HOUSE OF CARDS

Norwegian whistle-blower Boye Brogeland

Ron Schwartz (left) and Lotan Fisher

THE MAN WHO RIGGED THE LOTTERY

Eddie Tipton at his sentencing hearing in a Des Moines, Iowa, courthouse

I STARED DOWN DEATH

Clockwise, from top: Dennis McAninch's wrecked car in front of the Bigfoot store.
Tammi Smith, after her release; mother Cindy Hadix is on her right.
McAninch in an Ohio Department of Rehabilitation and Correction photo.

KILLER ON CALL

Nurse Charles Cullen (left) readily admitted to his crimes and pleaded guilty to killing 13 patients. He worked at ten hospitals and nursing homes over his 16-year career, including (clockwise from top left) Liberty Nursing and Rehabilitation Center in Allentown, Easton Hospital in Easton, St. Luke's Hospital in Bethlehem, and Sacred Heart Hospital in Allentown (all in Pennsylvania).

Left: The daughter and mother of victim Christopher Hardgrove watch the proceedings in a New Jersey courtroom. Right: Mary Strenko shows a photo of her son, murder victim Michael T. Strenko, outside the Somerset County Courthouse in Somerville, New Jersey.

HEIST

A little painting—Rembrandt's *Self Portrait*, above—caused big trouble for undercover agent Bob Wittman, a self-avowed keeper of the world's cultural flame. The painting was stolen in a daring theft from Sweden's Nationalmuseum in December 2000 and wasn't recovered until September 2005.

Brothers Baha and Dieya Kadhum were arrested twice and got off both times.

THE ALMOST-PERFECT MURDER

Clockwise, from left: The bloody hammer used to kill Donnah Winger;
Donnah's note about her frightening ride home from the airport with Roger Harrington
on the Wingers' refrigerator; Harrington's car

THE KILLER AMONG US

The Gustaf Adolph Evangelical Lutheran Church in New Sweden, Maine

THE KILLER AMONG US (CONTINUED)

Russell Kaye and Sandra Lee Phipps (2)

Investigators say the killer dropped a fistful of arsenic into the coffee urn.

A visiting pastor holds a photo of poisoning victim Reid Morrill, head usher at the church.

Russell Kaye and Sandra Lee Phipps

Members of the New Sweden community who drank the poisoned coffee, including Fran Ruggles (center front, wearing purple), Dick Ruggles (to her left), and Lester Beaupre (farthest left)

COLLARED

The attempted extortion of the Pulvers (Maddie, center, with her parents, Bill and Belinda) triggered an international manhunt from Australia to Louisville, Kentucky.

Paul Peters had left the financial industry
to write a novel about revenge.

CATCHING THE BTK KILLER

Dennis Rader, the BTK Killer

BTK clues were found on a rural road packed in a cereal box.

BTK's victims, top row, left to right: Julie and Joseph Otero, murdered in 1974; Kathryn Bright (1974). Bottom row: Nancy Fox (1977); Marine Hedge (1985); and Delores Davis (1991)

THE SEARCHER

Tim Tadder

James Spring near his home in San Diego

Left: Tim Tadder. Right: Courtesy James Spring

Viana (right) and Faith Carelli
inspired a stranger's quest to
do something meaningful.

Spring's poster was crucial
to locating the girls.

PARTNERS IN CRIME

A camera caught Craig Pritchert robbing a Norwest Bank branch in Scottsdale, Arizona, in 1997. His take: $32,000.

Nova Guthrie and Pritchert were arrested in South Africa in August 2003. Waiving extradition to the United States, they left separately after a final embrace.

KILLER CONNECTION

```
...that you are still writing a
...ssible they foresaw complicat:
...you signed the contract which y(
...ney should pay you something for the
...d. At least they could give you "mugg
...ave to go away empty handed. You said
...orry, I can't interpret the L.A. dialec
...ord: colloquialism. Does this mean that
...now, rabbits out of hats and things.
...uggest . . . a . . . ahmmm . . . that
...r carnally for a negotiated price? If
...n writing - it would almost have to -
...to administration or the actual delivery
...rse on your preferences and the opening:
...usiness loan to get started.

...me? Nothing that reincarnation won:
...to come back as Wes Ulhman, or (pe:
...Bridge. In short things could be
...about what is happening to me, I',
...captive audience. I'm supposed t:
...l on 14 counts involving the use of
...ngs.) Perfect time to use an insan
...televisions and, honest, I couldn't
...the Son of Sam SANE - which effecti
...ntry can be found legally insane - s
...lty defense, since, for the record a:
...nding this letter, I am innocent o.
...law and fact. CYA, my Dear.

...re, bon apetite, catch you later,
...s they talk to you first, down some
...on . . . .
                ted
```

Ted Bundy was author Ann Rule's partner at the Seattle Crisis Clinic,
where they fielded phone calls from strangers in emotional distress.
He wrote Rule several friendly but cagey letters from jail.

Bundy (left), a former law student, confers with his attorneys during his 1979 trial for the
murder of two Florida college students.
Right: A Seattle homicide unit displayed photos of his first six known victims (1974).

The first victims of Seattle's Green River Killer were found in the early 1980s, along the riverbanks. Many of the women (ten shown here) were not even 18 at the time they disappeared.

Left to right, from top row: Kimi-Kai Pitsor, Carol Ann Christensen, Wendy Lee Coffield, Patricia Yellow Robe, Constance Elizabeth Naon, Mary Bridget Meehan, Debra Bonner, Keli Kay McGinness, Marie M. Malvar, Cindy Smith

Carol Estes (left, with surviving daughter Virginia Graham) holds a portrait of her daughter Debra, one of at least 48 victims of Gary Ridgway (right), the Green River Killer.

TWO MILLION REASONS FOR MURDER

The body of April Barber (left) was found on an isolated beach south of Jacksonville, Florida. Her husband, Justin Barber (right), was arrested for her murder in 2004.

THE KILLER NEXT DOOR

Though Whitey Bulger landed in prison many times throughout his life, he was on the FBI's Most Wanted list for 16 years before being arrested for the final time, in 2011.

The Santa Monica apartment complex where Bulger and Josh Bond were neighbors

Fran Ruggles had a painful outbreak of shingles that lasted weeks. Dick still has back pain that might be nerve-related. And many survivors deal daily with crushing fatigue. Lester Beaupre was the last victim to be released from the hospital, almost five weeks after the poisoning. The tubes that kept him alive injured his throat, and he had a tracheotomy during his hospital stay. He still feels numbness in his face and extremities.

The community is also numb. "We're not innocent anymore," says Louise Beaupre. Healing, in every sense of the word, will take time. On a bright summer Sunday four months after the poisoning, victims were again gathering with their neighbors to pray at Gustaf Adolph church. Fran Ruggles helped serve communion as sunlight filtered through the church's stained-glass windows. Erich Margeson, Lester Beaupre and other victims recited from the Book of Psalms: "Who among you loves life and desires long life to enjoy prosperity?" At the bottom of the day's prayer list was the simple line "For the arsenic victims." And resting on the counter of the adjoining kitchen, plainly visible from the pews, was a new coffee urn.

It is an uncomfortable reminder of the tragedy, but more visceral is the knowledge that Danny Bondeson's accomplice could be in the next pew. That makes worship understandably difficult, even for the most forgiving of souls. Admits Lester Beaupre, "You look around at church and wonder who did it."

Fran Ruggles died in 2009 after struggling with health problems related to the poisoning. Dale Anderson still has neuropathy, and Lois Anderson suffers from memory loss and difficulty walking, side effects of arsenic poisoning.

"BETH'S BEEN KIDNAPPED!"

by Donald Robinson

On Thanksgiving weekend in 1976, 23-year-old Elizabeth (Beth) Ferringer was visiting her parents, Susan and Don Meyer, at their isolated home near State College, Pennsylvania. Because of his job, Beth's husband Michael had returned home early to Brookville, 81 miles away, and so he was not there when, on Sunday evening, Beth's harsh ordeal began.

Nor was her father. That evening, after a pleasant family dinner, Don Meyer had kissed his wife and daughter good night, and left for the Autoport, a motel-restaurant he owned in town. At 11:10 p.m., Susan Meyer was chatting on the telephone. Suddenly, the line went dead and the lights went out.

As the two women groped their way to the master bedroom for a kerosene lamp, there was a sound of shattering glass, then footsteps. Terrified, Beth and her mother pushed a chair against the bedroom door. Abruptly, the door was kicked in. A brawny man wearing a monster mask stood in the splintered entrance holding a pistol. Another masked gunman loomed behind him.

The men moved quickly. Forcing Susan Meyer to lie face-down on the floor, they tied her hands behind her back with nylon rope. "Don't call the police," they warned as they led Beth away, "or you'll never see your daughter alive again."

The kidnappers pulled a pillowcase over Beth's head,

then forced her into the back of her mother's Oldsmobile and drove off.

Soon after she heard the kidnappers leave, Susan Meyer managed to wriggle out of her bonds. She jumped into Beth's car and drove madly to the home of her nearest neighbor, nearly a half mile away. At 12:15 a.m. Don Meyer was told he had an urgent call from his wife.

"Beth's been kidnapped!" Susan sobbed. "They said they'll kill her if you call the police."

Meyer was stunned. He paced the floor, weighing alternatives. Then he decided there was only one thing to do.

* * *

Senior Resident Agent Tom Dolan, who headed the FBI office in State College, was asleep when the phone rang at 12:30 a.m., November 29. But the frantic voice of his friend, Don Meyer, pulled him from his slumber. My God, Dolan thought, Don's girl. I thought it only happened to strangers.

The agent's first step was to request a telephone company "trap"—which can trace a call in seconds by computer—on Meyer's Autoport phone. Then he notified FBI divisional headquarters in Philadelphia. Neil Welch, Special Agent in Charge, ordered 50 of his best agents to the scene. In 30 minutes he was on the road himself, driving the 195 miles to State College in sleet and snow.

* * *

At 2:25 a.m., Meyer's office phone rang. A male voice said in falsetto, "Do exactly what I say, or you'll never see your daughter alive again."

"What do you want?" Meyer asked.

"One hundred and fifty thousand dollars," the caller declared.

"Let me talk to Beth," Meyer begged.

"Impossible," the caller snapped, and hung up.

The call was traced to a phone booth on the outskirts of town.

An armed surveillance team was sent to watch the booth. But the only person to use it was a city policeman making a routine call to headquarters. Meanwhile, other FBI agents were converging on State College from their offices in Philadelphia, Harrisburg, Williamsport, Allentown and Scranton.

*   *   *

After a seemingly interminable drive, the Oldsmobile came to a stop. Beth was led into a musty building and down some stairs. A heavy chain was brutally cinched about her waist; it was attached to an overhead heating duct so tightly that she could scarcely move without pain. Near her feet were a roll of toilet paper, a jar of peanut butter, a moldy loaf of bread and a container of water.

"If everything goes our way," one of the men said, "we'll be back tonight."

*   *   *

Welch arrived at State College early Monday morning and began working out assignments. He posted agents to cover every major intersection, then told Ed Creasy, a 33-year-old FBI pilot, to go out to University Park Airport and rent a plane suitable for tailing. Creasy got a single-engined Cessna 150 with two seats.

The next call from the kidnappers came at 8:40 a.m. "Write this down," the falsetto voice told Meyer. "We want $25,000 in ten-dollar bills; $50,000 in twenties; $25,000 in fifties; and $50,000 in one hundreds. Put the money in an attaché case.

We want used bills with no consecutive serial numbers." The caller also directed Don to install a citizens band (CB) radio in his car.

Minutes later, the telephone company rang back. The trap had traced the call to a pay phone in the HUB—the Hetzel Union Building—on the Penn State campus. It was a clever choice by the kidnappers, for they could easily get in and out of this crowded student center without attracting attention.

* * *

As daylight penetrated the blackness of the cellar, Beth managed to remove the pillowcase from her head and saw and unused furnace and a partly empty coal bin. She could also see what had been making the scurrying noises through the night: small rodents scampered about her feet. Her teeth chattered from the numbing cold, her feet ached. She could hear cows mooing somewhere outside, but no human voices.

* * *

At 12:45 p.m., the voice on the phone asked, "Do you have the money?"

"It took too long getting the CB," Don Meyer replied. "As soon as we're finished with this call, I'll go to the bank. Let me speak to Beth."

"No," the voice said. "I'll call you at 4 p.m."

The trap traced the call to another pay phone at the HUB. Welch now made one of the most crucial decisions of the case. He gambled that the kidnappers would make their next call from the HUB as well, and drew his plans accordingly.

While Meyer drove to the Peoples National Bank to put up his house and business as security for a $150,000 loan, Welch selected ten agents who could pass as students or young instructors. Special Agent Dave Richter was in charge of the squad. Tall and blond, he looked ten years younger than his 33 years.

Singly and in pairs, the, casually attired FBI men sauntered over to the HUB, where eight phone booths stood near the front entrance. Richter sent agents into the first, third, sixth and seventh booths. An agent would be in the next booth no matter which one the kidnapper chose.

Shortly after 4 p.m., a stocky man strode into the HUB and went straight into the vacant booth next to Richter. As the agent pretended to make his own call, his heart jumped.

The man in the next booth was speaking in a falsetto voice.

"Go to the parking lot of the Bald Eagle Restaurant in Milesburg," the man instructed (Milesburg is 13 miles north of State College). "Turn on your overhead light and switch your CB to Channel 7."

Richter excitedly phoned the command post. "I have the guy. He's speaking to Don Meyer now. I'm going to tail him."

The man hung up, then walked casually to a brown late-model Pontiac in the HUB parking lot. By bizarre coincidence, it was parked next to Richter's car.

The Pontiac was registered to the Two Wheels Cycle Shop in State College. "Hold on!" exclaimed Ernest Neil, a local FBI man. "That's Gary Young's place." Gary R. Young, the 33-year-old owner of the motorcycle shop, and his 23-year-old brother, Kent, who worked for him, were not unknown to the police: they were awaiting sentencing on a recent conviction of aggravated assault and recklessly endangering another person.

The safe course for Welch would have been to pick up Gary Young and hope that he talked. But Beth Ferringer's life was in danger. Welch decided to go through with the ransom payoff and hope that Gary would lead them to his captive.

* * *

*Daylight was fading. The kidnappers should be returning soon.
Suddenly she heard a loud crash. They've come back, she thought.
But the noise had been caused by winds that blew in the boards
covering a broken window. The inside temperature dropped,
leaving Beth numb with cold, but she refused to give up hope.*

* * *

Don Meyer drove to Milesburg, parked at the Bald Eagle and
turned on his overhead light. The CB in the station wagon
sounded: "Dome Light, do you read me?" Meyer said he did,
and was ordered to drive to the Nittany Mall shopping center. As he drove, he switched off the overhead light—and the
CB barked, "Turn that light back on." Meyer realized with a
start that the kidnappers' car was right behind him. The light
would keep him from glimpsing any faces.

As Meyer turned into Nittany Mall, the CB ordered: "Go
back toward State College." The directions then came, like
machine-gun fire. Turn right on Puddintown Road. Take a left
on Houserville Road. Proceed to Airport Road. The kidnappers were zigzagging, trying to shake off any followers. They
didn't succeed. The surveillance squad—six unmarked cars,
alternating as the tail—was on target.

Following orders, Meyer turned onto a narrow road that ran
into the woods. It turned to dirt and meandered into a desolate,
snow-covered cornfield. The kidnappers' car was nowhere in
sight, but the voice on the CB crackled: "Leave the case."

Meyer opened the door and placed the attaché case in the
middle of the road. Then he headed back toward State College.

The most critical time in any kidnapping is after the ransom has been dropped off. If the kidnappers suspect that the

police are closing in, they may abandon the loot and kill the victim. Welch gambled again. He called off the surveillance squad and left it to Ed Creasy to follow the car from above.

In the meantime, agents Joseph McQuillan and Austin Hamilton, only three-eighths of a mile from the scene, were ordered to cut through the heavy woods to a spot where they could observe the pickup. Their eyewitness testimony would be important to any prosecution. Almost a half hour passed. Then the Pontiac pulled up alongside the attaché case. Gary Young reached out, picked up the case and drove off.

*   *   *

At 6:30 p.m., Don Meyer returned to the Autoport. Suddenly, everything seemed to collapse. Gary Young telephoned in a wild rage. He'd spotted the plane. "You blew it! You got airplane surveillance on us," he screamed.

"What the hell are you talking about?" Meyer yelled back. "There isn't any plane. You have the money. Please, tell me where Beth is!"

Gary subsided. "I'll call you in an hour," he said.

The kidnappers didn't call in an hour. Nor in two hours. "Please, God," Meyer prayed. "Let them call."

The Young brothers drove back to the motorcycle shop, stayed a while and drove out again. By 9 p.m., the FBI plane had been airborne more than four hours. It landed at 9:15 p.m., with two-tenths of a gallon of gas left in the tank.

Before they came down, Creasy signaled the auto-surveillance squad to resume the tail by flashing his lights—lights that Gary Young spotted. Panicked, Young phoned the airport. By sheer good luck, Creasy answered. When Young demanded to know if any policeman were flying, he answered, "Nope, just a student pilot with an instructor."

"But this plane kept turning its lights on and off," Young insisted.

Creasy reacted coolly: "The student probably grabbed the wrong buttons in the dark. Happens all the time."

Young fell for it. At 10 p.m. he telephoned the Autoport and told Don where to find Beth. "Take a hacksaw with you," he said.

*   *   *

As Welch ordered his surveillance teams to move in on the kidnappers—"But no arrests yet"—Beth's parents, her husband Mike and her father-in-law raced to free her. A string of FBI cars tore after them, and they all screeched to a halt near an abandoned frame house 23 miles from State College.

Ernest Neil and a state trooper broke down the cellar door and found Beth shivering on the dirt floor. The water the kidnappers had left her was frozen solid; the temperature was only two degrees above zero. A few more hours, Welch thought, and she would have frozen to death.

In tears, Beth grabbed Mike. Then her father and father-in-law were hugging her. In the cold outside, Beth's mother waited anxiously. Welch had refused to let her in. He didn't know what they would find.

An FBI agent sawed off Beth's chains. She had no feeling in her legs and could barely walk. Don and Mike quickly bundled her into the warm car. Soon Beth was safely back in her parents' home. The ordeal was over.

*   *   *

Gary Young was driving alone when FBI agents forced his car off the road and, guns drawn, arrested him. Five other agents hit Kent's apartment, and seized him in his bedroom. The next morning FBI agents found the ransom money hidden in an olive-drab laundry bag under six inches of insulation in Gary Young's attic.

To the FBI's deep regret, the kidnappers could not be prosecuted under federal law—which provides for life imprisonment—since neither brother crossed state lines in the commission of the crime. Both Youngs were sentenced to terms in the Pennsylvania State Correctional Institution. Gary received a ten- to twenty-year sentence, Kent eight to twenty years.

Gary Young was released on parole in 1990 after serving thirteen years of his ten- to twenty-year sentence. Kent Young was released on parole in 1983 after serving six years of an eight- to twenty-year sentence.

COLLARED!

by Simon Bouda

Sitting in her bedroom in her parents' spacious Sydney, Australia, home, Maddie Pulver contemplated the task ahead—studying. It was August 3, 2011, and high school exams were coming up. Like her classmates, she was hitting the books.

It was 2:30 p.m., a Wednesday, and the 18-year-old was alone in the house. Maddie's mother was out shopping, and her father, the CEO of a global software company, was at work; her two younger brothers were at school, and her older brother was on vacation. From her bedroom desk, Maddie could gaze out across Sydney Harbor, but this was a time for concentration, not daydreaming.

Suddenly, Maddie heard a noise behind her. She turned to find a man standing in her bedroom doorway wearing a rainbow-colored balaclava. He was armed with an aluminum baseball bat and wore a small black backpack. The intruder had entered the multimillion-dollar home through the un-locked front door.

"I am not going to hurt you," he declared.

Maddie leaped from her chair and backed away, toward her bed. "What do you want?" she demanded.

Placing his baseball bat and backpack on the bed, the man simply warned, "No one needs to get hurt."

He opened the backpack and removed a black metal box the size of a small laptop. Holding it against Maddie's throat, he secured it around her neck with a bicycle lock. He then placed a loop of purple string over her head. Attached to it were a USB flash drive and a plastic sleeve with a document inside. A label with a typed e-mail address, dirkstruan1840@gmail.com, was stuck to the box around her neck.

Turning to leave, the man told Maddie to "count to 200. I'll be back. If you move, I can see you. I'll be right here."

Terrified, Maddie remained still. After a few moments, she called out for help. Silence. She called out again. Nothing.

With the device strapped to her neck, Maddie moved slowly toward her cell phone. Without daring to jolt the contraption, she texted her mother and father, asking them to call the police. Only then did Maddie remove the document from the plastic sleeve attached to the string. When she glimpsed the word *explosives*, she burst into tears.

"Powerful new technology plastic explosives are located inside the small black combination case delivered to you," read the letter. "The case is booby-trapped. It can ONLY be opened safely if you follow the instructions. If you disclose these Instructions to any Federal or State agency, the Police or FBI, or to any nonfamily member, it will trigger an immediate BRIAN DOUGLAS WELLS event. You will be provided with detailed Remittance Instructions to transfer a Defined Sum once you acknowledge and confirm receipt of this message. If the Remittance Instructions are executed CORRECTLY, I will immediately provide you with the combination that can open the case WITHOUT triggering a BRIAN DOUGLAS WELLS event and an internal key to completely disable the explosive mechanisms embedded inside. CONFIRM receipt of these Instructions by CONTACTING: dirkstruan1840@ gmail.com."

Brian Douglas Wells was a pizza deliveryman duped by a gang in 2003 in Pennsylvania. They put a collar time bomb around his neck and ordered him to rob a bank. Wells did as he was told, but when he was leaving the bank, police turned up. The bomb went off with catastrophic consequences.

But Maddie Pulver had no idea what a "Brian Douglas Wells event" was. She was also unaware that Dirk Struan—the name used for the e-mail address—was the main character in James Clavell's novel *Tai-Pan*.

Struan was the "Tai-Pan"—the leader—a wealthy, violent, and shrewd head of a trading company in China who was hell-bent on destroying his rivals.

*   *   *

The Australian police had never seen a case like this before. Arriving soon after 2:45 p.m., officers immediately sealed off the street and set up roadblocks to divert traffic, curious neighbors, and the media.

Inside the house, they found Maddie sobbing. To take the weight off her neck, she was holding the box with her hands. Police had kept her parents at a mobile command post out on the street, so Constable Karen Lowden took on the task of trying to comfort the terrified teen. She asked about the up-coming exams, Maddie's art studies, her hobbies . . . anything to keep their minds off the horrible predicament while bomb squad technicians determined what sort of explosive they were dealing with. Portable X-ray equipment showed that the box was filled with mechanical and electrical components. But police couldn't be sure if there were explosives or not.

Meanwhile, the police decided to respond to the extortionist and carefully crafted a short, simple reply, which Maddie's father would send. At around 6 p.m., he e-mailed the address attached to the black metal box: "Hi, my name is Bill. I am the father of the girl you strapped the device to. What do you want me to do next?"

As police and Maddie's family waited for a reply that never came, the extortion note was sent through forensic examination for fingerprints, and detectives questioned neighbors and friends, trying to piece together what had happened.

Then at 11:00—a breakthrough. After analyzing X-rays and receiving advice from military experts, the bomb squad concluded that the device did not contain explosives and posed no threat. The collar bomb was cut off Maddie. Her nearly nine hours of hell were over.

But where was the would-be extortionist?

*   *   *

Almost immediately after being handed the note, police contacted Google's head office in the United States to determine if the Gmail account had been accessed. The Internet giant scanned its database records and told detectives that the account, dirkstruan1840@gmail.com, had been created on May 30 from an Internet server linked to Chicago's O'Hare Airport.

That night, Google's data revealed the e-mail account had been logged on to three times that afternoon—twice from a computer at a library a few hours north of Sydney and a third time from a nearby video store.

Because Google could tell the detectives the precise times someone had used the account, police were able to view the library's parking lot security video and pinpoint the arrival of a possible suspect and the car he was driving, a metallic gold

Range Rover. Although the license plates were illegible, detectives had an image of the man who'd gotten out of the SUV and entered the library.

Maddie had told police her attacker wasn't young. She had noticed gray chest hair as he reached around her to attach the collar box. Through the eyeholes in his balaclava, she'd seen wrinkles. She'd guessed he was between 55 and 60. The man in the video fit the description and wore a collared shirt and trousers similar to what Maddie remembered.

Then, by checking motor vehicle records, they systematically checked the registration details of each possible Range Rover with driver's license photos of their owners. Within 48 hours of getting hold of the library footage, they had a name—Paul Douglas Peters.

With that name, detectives were able to follow a money trail, providing more links to the crime. Peters's bank records showed that he'd made purchases at a clothing and sporting goods store in the weeks before Maddie was attacked. Footage from the shopping center showed him buying a baseball bat and a rainbow-colored balaclava.

Police also learned that Peters had degrees in economics and law; he was a businessman, father of three, and self-proclaimed author. He'd planned the elaborate extortion piece by piece, like writing a novel.

They had enough to bring him in for questioning, except for one thing—Peters had already fled the country. Security footage and immigration records showed the 52-year-old Australian passing through Sydney Airport en route to Los Angeles on August 8. Flight records showed Peters then caught a connecting flight to Chicago, before flying to Louisville, Kentucky.

Twelve days after the attack on Maddie, on August 15, an

FBI team stormed the Kentucky home of Peters's ex-wife, where they found Peters. There on a table was a James Clavell novel—*Tai-Pan*.

Detective Sergeant Andrew Marks flew from Australia to Louisville to question Peters. In a room at FBI headquarters, he chipped away at the suspect.

Marks: "Is there anything you want to tell me about the extortion, the kidnapping, and the bomb placed around young Madeleine Pulver's neck on the third of August?"

Peters: "No."

Marks: "Are you responsible?"

Peters: "No."

Marks: "Do you know anything about an e-mail address with that name, Dirk Struan?"

Peters: "Yes."

Marks: "What can you tell me about that?"

Peters: "I had a . . . or had set up an e-mail address with . . . Dirk Struan."

Marks then asked about the USB flash drive that had been attached to the collar bomb. Forensic examination had unearthed three deleted files. One was a Word file that was a letter of demand in the same terms as the saved file and the hard-copy document in the plastic sleeve placed around Maddie's neck. The analysis of the Word file revealed that it had been created on a computer identified as "Paul P."

Peters was unable to explain why or how the document had been on a "Paul P" computer. He claimed it was "a horrible, horrible coincidence."

During questioning, Peters talked about a James M. Cox Trust, claiming he had $12 million tied up in it. Another of the three deleted files on the USB drive contained a letter of demand addressed specifically to the trustee of the trust.

It indicated that perhaps Maddie wasn't the intended target of the extortion plan, that the masked intruder had meant to target a neighbor who was a beneficiary of the trust. Marks handed Peters a copy of the deleted document.

Marks: "Have you seen that note before?"

Peters: "I have no comment."

* * *

Paul Douglas Peters was soon on a plane back to Australia to face charges of aggravated breaking and entry and kidnapping. Despite his initial denials, Peters pleaded guilty to the crime, although he never did explain why he targeted Maddie.

During the sentencing, the prosecutor described the extortion attempt as "urban terrorism, which would strike fear into the heart of every parent." But Peters's legal team tried to build a case suggesting that he was suffering a psychotic episode at the time he attacked Maddie. They insisted Peters had become obsessed with a novel he'd been writing and was "living" the role of a main character.

Forensic psychiatrists agreed that Peters did suffer depression and overused alcohol after the collapse of his business and his divorce. One said he had a bipolar disorder.

But the judge wasn't convinced.

"The weight of evidence establishes beyond reasonable doubt that the offender set into action a plan to extort money," Judge Peter Zahra said. "There are limitations to which the extent of the terror experienced by the victim can be humanly understood."

A year after his arrest, Peters was sentenced to 13 years and six months in prison.

Outside the court, Maddie faced the media.

"I am pleased with today's outcome and that I can now look

to a future without Paul Peters's name being linked to mine," Maddie said. "For me, it was never about the sentencing but to know he will not reoffend, and it was good to hear the judge acknowledge the trauma he's put my family and me through."

It's a saga her mother, Belinda, sums up best: "We've realized what's important in life. We don't worry about the small things now."

CATCHING THE BTK KILLER

by Max Alexander

Something doesn't seem right, thought Cindy Plant as her truck bounced along an old dirt road north of Wichita in January 2005. Plant, 52, is code and animal control officer for the tiny community of Valley Center, which lies just north of the country road. Valley Center has many paved highways, but Cindy prefers North Seneca Street, a less traveled agricultural route that parts a sea of wheat fields.

She was taking Seneca to Park City, a nearby town where her friend Dennis Rader held the same position she did. They'd met in 1991 when Plant, a sturdy blonde with a soft open face, trained Rader in animal control—teaching him how to recognize and evaluate dog behavior, when to use the tranquilizer gun, and how to deal with sadness when dogs need to be put down.

The back of Plant's truck is often populated with a barking dog or two, generally in some state of distress, but today what distracted her was litter—specifically a Post Toasties cereal box propped up against a road-curve signpost. As a code officer, Plant pays attention to trash. "If I see tires dumped, or an old freezer, I get out and report it to Environmental Health," she says. "When you look at trash and debris, it's flung, it's thrown, it's blown, but it's never propped up." Plant passed the box for several days, curious yet always too busy to get out and take a look.

As Plant suspected, the cereal box was not trash. It had been weighted with a brick and positioned carefully against the signpost by Wichita's notorious serial killer, who in a letter to police once referred to himself as BTK—short for "bind them, toture [sic] them, kill them."

BTK enjoyed corresponding with the cops, sometimes via the media. In a postcard tip sent to a local TV station about the time Plant spotted the cereal box, the killer indicated its location, and said the box contained a doll, some jewelry, and an "acronym list" that may have been a word puzzle.

Months earlier, the reemergence of BTK, who had not been heard from in 25 years, had sent shock waves through Wichita. Police believed he was responsible for some ten deaths, his reign of terror beginning on January 15, 1974, when he murdered Joseph Otero and his family.

After serving 20 years in the Air Force, Otero, 38, had moved with his wife, Julie, 34, and their five children to Wichita, a center of aircraft manufacturing. The killer apparently interrupted a sandwich-making operation when he entered the modest Otero home on that cold winter morning: In the kitchen, a knife coated in peanut butter was found in mid-smear on a slice of bread. The telephone line had been cut. BTK tied up Joseph, Julie and two of their children—Joey, 9, and Josie, 11—then, according to police reports, slowly strangled them to death with venetian blind cords. Although he did not sexually assault any of the victims, semen was found on young Josie's inner thigh, indicating the killer was a sociopath who took sexual pleasure in the killing.

He also took souvenirs—a watch and a key chain—leaving the bodies to be discovered by the couple's other three children, all teenagers, when hours later they returned home from school.

Determined to solve the Otero crime quickly, police mobilized across town, interviewing anyone who had even a remote acquaintance with the victims. They set up a roadblock near the house and quizzed passing drivers. Wichita Police Chief Floyd Hannon even traveled to the Oteros' native Puerto Rico as well as Panama, where the family had once been stationed, looking for clues. In the ensuing months several arrests were made, but the suspects all had good alibis and were released. Because DNA matching had yet to be developed, the killer's semen sample was of little help in the investigation.

*　*　*

The Otero family was killed when Dennis Rader was 28 and between jobs. His father, William, who died in 1996, was a former Marine who worked at a Wichita power plant; mother Dorothea was a grocery store bookkeeper and still lives in the Park City bungalow where Dennis and his three younger brothers grew up—on North Seneca Street, a couple of miles south of where the Post Toasties box was found.

John Davis, 59, Rader's best friend from age five, recalls enjoying a Tom Sawyer–Huck Finn childhood with his pal. "We spent a lot of time at the Little Arkansas River, fishing and swimming," he says. "We would dig foxholes and build forts. Neither of us ever got into any sort of trouble. Our parents kept a close eye on us. Dennis's father was a very nice person. He was fair-minded, but you just knew he didn't put up with any nonsense." The pair joined the Boy Scouts, regularly taking long hikes and canoe trips.

After graduation from Wichita's Heights High School in 1963, Davis saw less of Rader, but the friends remained loyal. "He would lend me his car so I could pursue my girlfriend," says Davis, who is a staff member at the University of Washington in Seattle. When that girlfriend became Davis's wife in 1966, Rader was best man. The same year, Rader joined the Air Force. After an honorable discharge in 1970, he married Paula Dietz and settled down in Park City to raise a family in a small '50s ranch house they purchased on Independence Street, a crescent-shaped lane with no sidewalks.

Until July 1973, Rader worked as an assembler at the local Coleman camping supply factory. In November 1974 he landed a position as an installer for ADT, the nationwide home security company. The job was the first in a series of positions that gave Rader access to Wichita homes in an official capacity.

*   *   *

Three months after the Otero murders, the killer struck again—stabbing to death 21-year-old Kathryn Bright, a worker at Coleman, and shooting her brother Kevin, who escaped with serious head injuries. It was just a few months after the Bright murder that the killer first identified himself as BTK in a grammatically challenged, typewritten letter to police. "I'm sorry this happen to society," he wrote. "They are the ones who suffer the most. It's hard for me to control myself. You probably call me 'psychotic with sexual perversion hang-up.' When this monster enter my brain, I will never know."

To prove his authenticity, the killer related details of the Otero murders that had not been released to the public: "All victims had their hands tie nehind [sic] their backs. Gags of pillow case material. Slip knotts [sic] on Joe and Joseph . . . Purse contents south of the table. Spilled drink in that area also, kids making lunches."

More grim killings, and letters, were to come. On Saint Patrick's Day of 1977, BTK entered the tidy cottage of a 24-year-old church choir singer named Shirley Vian, locked her three children in the bathroom, and then tied Vian to a bed and strangled her as the children wailed. "They were very lucky," BTK wrote in a letter. "A phone call save them. I was going to tape the boys and put plastics bag over there [sic] head like I did Joseph [Otero] and Shirley. And then hang the girl. God-oh God what a beautiful sexual relief that would [have] been."

In December of the same year, not far from Vian's home, BTK bound and strangled Nancy Fox, a 25-year-old secretary; then he used a downtown pay phone to report the homicide. "You had to have lived here to know the fear that gripped this city," recalls Plant. "The Otero killings happened on my 21st birthday. I was a young mother and just scared to death." Robert Beattie, a local lawyer and author of a book about BTK called *Nightmare in Wichita*, says a generation of Wichita women took to checking their phone lines the moment they entered their homes.

*   *   *

In 1975, after BTK had killed five people, Rader's son, Brian, was born. When Paula Rader was pregnant again, in January 1978, BTK claimed responsibility for killing Shirley Vian in a poem called "Shirleylocks," based on the nursery rhyme "Curley Locks," that he sent to the Wichita newspaper. Ten days later he sent another poem to a local TV station in which he described killing Nancy Fox. "Seven down and many more to go," he warned. Four months later, Kerri Rader was born.

*   *   *

During those years, Rader attended Wichita State University— graduating in 1979 with a degree in administration of justice, which typically leads to a career in law enforcement.

At the same time, Arlyn Smith, a young Wichita detective,

hoped to trace the killer through the physical evidence of his letters. BTK usually sent police poor photocopies of the original letters, to distort the typewriter's "fingerprint." But Smith figured even photocopies must have some identifiable characteristics. The Xerox Corporation, along with paper and toner manufacturers, agreed to help. Thanks to their efforts, some of BTK's letters were traced to two copy machines on the Wichita State campus.

Police had located the haystack, but they still had to find the needle.

Then, after seven victims, the letters and killings stopped. As the years went by, many assumed BTK had died, moved away or been imprisoned, but Wichita's new police chief, Richard LaMunyon, wasn't so sure. In 1984, LaMunyon launched a task force to investigate the crimes. To avoid tipping off the complacent killer, the force was kept secret and named Ghostbusters after that spring's hit movie. It included local psychologist John Allen, who began poring over the history of the case.

"When I reviewed the 1970s investigations," recalls Allen, "it became apparent that they were looking for an obvious madman—someone who would act so bizarre that he drew attention to himself. But I believed you could be next to this guy in an elevator and have no idea. I felt he was thoroughly ensconced in a social network—his job, his church."

By the mid-'80s, DNA was beginning to be used in criminal forensics, so the Ghostbusters began voluntary DNA testing of suspects. They used computer databases to scan records at Wichita State, hoping to cross-reference a suspect. They even convinced the Pentagon to let them view top-secret military satellite photos of Wichita on crime days. Still no killer. LaMunyon disbanded the Ghostbusters in 1986, and the trail went cold.

* * *

In 1988, Dennis Rader left ADT. The following year he became the Wichita field operations supervisor for the 1990 Census. Among his jobs was verifying new residential addresses around town. In 1991 he became the uniformed code officer for Park City. He also wore the uniform of a Scout leader, working with a local pack of which his son, Brian, was a member.

In Park City, Rader gained a reputation as a stickler for the rules. "He came out and measured my grass and said it was too long," remembers Cheryl Hooten, owner of Auntie C's, a local restaurant. "He fined me for putting up [restaurant] signs around town. I had no inkling they weren't allowed."

Cindy Plant says Rader's personal appearance reflected his attention to detail: "You never saw him in blue jeans; he wore Dockers and nice shirts. His desk was immaculate, everything hung up on a pinboard." Plant traveled all over the state with Rader, organizing training seminars. They stayed in hotels and spent hours in the car and over meals, but Rader never talked much about his personal life. "One time he had just taken his kids on a vacation and seemed to be thrilled about it," she says. "I could tell he really cared about his family." Although Plant never saw him lose control, there were stories. She once heard that Rader "blew up at the Wichita animal shelter manager for changing their billing practice."

George Martin, a fellow Cub Scout leader, says that Rader was a stickler with his young Scouts. He recalls that Rader took his outdoor skills seriously. "He taught the boys knots," Martin says. "He was very strict that they learn; he wouldn't let them slack off."

* * *

In January 2004 the *Wichita Eagle* ran a story marking the 30th anniversary of the unsolved Otero murders. Two months later, the newspaper received a letter with a return address of Bill Thomas Killman (initials BTK). In the envelope was a photocopy of a driver's license belonging to Vicki Wegerle, a 28-year-old Wichita mother who'd been strangled in 1986, and three photos of the death scene apparently taken by the killer. The unsolved Wegerle murder had not been linked to BTK, but based on characteristics of the letter, police were certain this was no copycat. After 25 years of silence, BTK was back.

While a new generation of Wichitans checked their phones and nervously eyed strangers, the killer fired off at least eight separate communications over the next 11 months—daring police with word puzzles, dolls, and chapters of his proposed autobiography. With his taunting letters and sick poems, "he seemed to take a special enjoyment out of proving the cops couldn't catch him," says Dr. Allen, the Wichita psychologist. "He was obviously a very narcissistic guy who sought a lot of attention."

Assuming BTK was at least in his 20s when he killed the Oteros, he would have to be more than 50 by now. But if he had changed over the years, so had the tools to catch him. On February 16, 2005, a local TV station received a padded envelope from BTK containing a necklace and a copy of the cover of a novel about a killer who bound and gagged his victims. The package also contained a computer disc. Investigators were able to recover deleted files on the disc that suggested it had been used at the Christ Lutheran Church near Park City. The recently elected president of the church council at Christ Lutheran, police learned, was Dennis Rader, 59-year-old married father of two grown children—a balding, bespectacled Cub Scout leader and former Wichita State University student.

At some point, police had secretly obtained a sample of 26-year-old Kerri Rader's DNA, probably through medical lab records. It was reported that the sample closely matched DNA from one or more of the original crime scenes.

Rader was arrested on February 25, 2005, as he drove near his home. He is said to have confessed to a total of 10 murders, including the 1985 killing of Marine Hedge, a 53-year-old widow who lived on Rader's block. The last known murder was in 1991, when BTK abducted 62-year-old grandmother Delores Davis from her home, just up the road from Christ Lutheran Church.

*   *   *

Carmen Montoya was in her Albuquerque office when a Wichita detective called with the news. Montoya is a 45-year-old mother who works for a nonprofit group that mentors school kids. Her maiden name is Otero. On a winter day in Wichita in 1974, 13-year-old Carmen skipped home from school to discover her strangled parents in their bedroom. She was raised by family friends.

When the detective called, "I was speechless," Montoya says in a soft, clear voice. "I felt relieved, angry and sad. I thought [the killer] would be a really big, mean-looking man. It blows me away that this was a man who was so active in his church."

She wasn't alone. Cindy Plant has a hard time forming complete sentences when she talks about Rader now. Standing outside the animal shelter in Valley Center, on a late winter afternoon, she ignores a chorus of yelping dogs and scans the sky, as if the right words might flash like falling stars. "We stayed in hotels, had dinner together. And to find out that the person I've lived in fear of all these years was . . . My God, I haven't just known a killer. I think I could deal with that. But

I've known someone who was a serial killer. You wonder what makes these types of people tick."

Like many who knew Rader, childhood friend John Davis speculates that he had more than one personality, each unaware of the others. But Dr. James Alan Fox, coauthor of *Extreme Killing: Understanding Serial and Mass Murder*, says that assumption, while comforting to those who knew the "good" Dennis, is probably off the mark. "Lots of people have multiple sides of the same personality," he says. "It's not schizophrenic, but they are able to compartmentalize. Serial killers can be good husbands and fathers and neighbors, but strangers mean nothing to them."

Davis wants to visit Rader in the Sedgwick County jail, where he is being held on $10 million bond. "If I sat down with him I would say, 'I'm here to see the Dennis that I know and care about, but there's another part of you that I don't understand.'" He fumbles and fights back tears. "And I would just ask him, 'What the hell were you thinking?'"

Fox says a killer like BTK is typically obsessed with power and control. "It's probably not a coincidence that the killings stopped when Rader got the position as compliance officer," he explains, adding that the motivation for serial killers is fairly straightforward. "Lots of people take pleasure in other people's pain. At lower levels we see it in people who are sarcastic." Serial killers take that to the extreme, of course, and understanding why is not so easy. Fox speculates that such killers have particularly vivid sexual fantasies that they feel compelled to pursue. Once they kill, says Fox, "the fantasies become crystallized and more demanding."

It's all academic to those who know Rader. "I try not to understand him," says Christ Lutheran Pastor Michael Clark, "because then I might judge him."

On May 3, Rader, now 60, stood mute at his arraignment and allowed the judge to enter a plea of not guilty on his behalf. He awaits trial on charges that would bring life in prison. (Because the BTK murders were committed before 1994, when Kansas reinstated the death penalty, the charges are not capital-punishment offenses.)

* * *

Two Sundays before Easter and two weeks after Rader's arrest, bright morning sun streams through the high windows of Christ Lutheran Church. Paula Rader's seat in the choir remains empty; until recently a bookkeeper for a local convenience store, she remains in seclusion. Their daughter, Kerri, is married to a Web designer and lives in Michigan. Son Brian is in the Naval Submarine School in Connecticut.

Assisting Minister Donn Bischoff offers a prayer "for the Rader family and for the victims of BTK and their families." The Gospel reading is the story of Lazarus, whom Christ brought back from the dead. Jesus tells his disciples, "Those who walk during the day do not stumble, because they see the light of this world. But those who walk at night stumble, because the light is not in them."

After the service, Pastor Clark removes his vestments and sighs wearily. "Nothing in the seminary prepared me for this," he says. Clark is a year older than Rader. Three times a week, he drives down to the jail and speaks with his congregant from the other side of a glass wall. "He needs a pastor," adds Clark. "And the family is devastated. Paula's life is turned upside down. I'm afraid she may have to move away, because people will take it out on her."

Or they may take it out on Clark himself. "Some people want me to get up on that pulpit and condemn Dennis to hell," he remarks. "But that's not why I was called into the ministry."

All the while, Cindy Plant can't stop thinking about the cereal box. "Now BTK was a puzzle and a game person," she says. "And you know how that box was against a road-curve sign? Well, the arrow on that sign points to Park City. I keep wondering if that was a clue."

Carmen Montoya is looking toward the future; she plans to attend Rader's trial. "At this point I don't even know if I could face him, but I feel I need to," she says. "He got gratification ruining people's lives. He needs to know that he didn't ruin mine."

Dennis Rader was sentenced to ten consecutive life terms. He is incarcerated in Kansas's El Dorado Correctional Facility.

THE SEARCHER

by Joe Rhodes

The girl in the photo had wide eyes and a princess smile, blond hair, a strand of plastic pearls dangling from her neck. James Spring felt a pang in his heart the moment he saw her on his computer screen. She looked so happy and innocent, so much like his own daughter, Addie, who was tucked in upstairs. When he saw the picture and read what had happened to six-year-old Viana and her infant sister, Faith, he knew what he had to do.

His 40th birthday, on April 29, was just a few weeks away, and Spring was looking to keep a promise to himself. He'd been restless the past few months, distracted by the fear that he'd settled a little too easily into middle age. He was successful and proud of the life he had built: the marketing job in San Diego, the spacious house in the La Mesa suburbs, the loving wife, the two wonderful kids—three-year-old Addie and eight-month-old Caden. But it didn't feel like enough.

When he was younger, he'd been a danger junkie, reporting on civil wars in El Salvador and Guatemala for National Public Radio, getting himself captured by Kuna Indians and pursued by paramilitary gangs. "I had an inflated sense of my own invulnerability," he says now.

If he hadn't met Kellie, the woman he married six years ago, he'd probably still be coming up against shady characters. But she convinced him—made an ultimatum of it, actually—that if he was going to be her husband and the father of her children, he couldn't go dashing into any more war zones. He fed his need for adventure by scuba diving and racing his motorcycle in the Baja 500. And then, his birthday approaching, he started talking about doing something that would make him feel better about himself.

"Maybe there will be an earthquake and I can dig people out of the rubble," he told Kellie. "Or a helicopter will go down and they'll need people to search." She tried to ignore him, hoping he'd forget about his quest and just have a party in the backyard. But he wouldn't let it go. "I told her, 'I just want to do something that's going to help somebody else.'"

Which is why James Spring was looking up missing-person cases on the Internet in early April, hoping to find someone who needed him. When he saw that photo and started reading about Viana and Faith Carelli, two girls who'd been taken away by their parents—convicts who were suspects in a San Francisco murder, didn't have legal custody of their older daughter, and had last been seen by a tourist in the Baja peninsula—it became clear what his birthday gift to himself would be. He was going to load up his Ford Explorer, drive across the border, and go looking for those two little girls.

*　*　*

The house in Soquel, California, where Gene and Ellen Pauly have lived for 32 years is overflowing with photos of their family: the five children they raised together, the foster kids they took in, the grandkids, including Viana and Faith.

Most of the photos of their daughter Michele, Viana and Faith's mother, were taken during her high school years, when everyone called her the golden child. A cheerleader, a ballet and tap dancer, the president of Students Against Drunk Driving, she was the pretty one, the popular one, the daughter every parent hoped to have. She graduated from Aptos High School in 1988, spent six months with a performance group in Japan, and earned a dance education degree from Western Kentucky University.

Ellen Pauly, 63, still doesn't understand what happened to that Michele. She doesn't recognize the woman her daughter, now 39, has become: a meth user, a thief, a con artist, possibly an accessory to murder. "I still love my daughter," she says, "but she's not the Michele we raised. Whether that Michele can ever come back again, it's hard to tell. I'm not counting on it."

Maybe there were problems all along; maybe her parents just didn't know. But there's no question that Michele's life took a turn for the worse after she left Soquel. In 1994 she married Joe Pinkerton, a ski instructor she'd met while working as a dancer in Lake Tahoe. She moved to Los Angeles and started spending time with Pinkerton's friend Richard Carelli. Eight years into the marriage, she left Pinkerton and moved in with Carelli. The two drifted from one dead-end job to another.

The Paulys know little of Carelli's life before he met Michele, other than that he'd had odd jobs, occasionally tending bar or working construction. The Paulys say he could be charming but also frightening. And, they say, he seemed to have an almost hypnotic effect on their daughter.

"Richard was the one who destroyed Michele," says Gene Pauly, 76, sounding more sad than angry. She would disappear from her parents' lives for years at a time. When she surfaced, she was hostile, resentful, usually asking for money.

Ellen is convinced that she might not have seen much of Viana if Michele hadn't been broke in 2004. But Michele needed help taking care of her then-three-year-old daughter, so she moved into her parents' house and told them she'd left Carelli. She got a job. Things looked promising.

And they were—until a few weeks later, when Carelli showed up and took Michele and Viana away. The couple fell into the same patterns as before and soon racked up convictions for drug possession and arrests for petty theft and credit card fraud. The final straw for the Paulys came in December 2006, when police burst into a motel room in nearby Capitola to arrest Carelli and Michele. Meth was scattered on the nightstand; Viana, age four, was found hiding under the bed.

Gene and Ellen Pauly petitioned for custody of their granddaughter and won. But over the Paulys' objections, a judge granted Carelli and Michele the right to unsupervised visits. Viana often spent weekends with her parents and their new baby, Faith, born in October 2007 with Down syndrome.

At the start of one of those weekends, in January 2008, Ellen noticed that something didn't seem right. Michele appeared more scattered than usual as she scooped up her daughter's overnight bag and went off into the rainy afternoon. Ellen had a bad feeling—but no way of knowing it would be ten weeks before she would see Viana again.

*　*　*

Until that day, Carelli and Michele had been living in San Francisco's Mission Terrace neighborhood, renting a one-bedroom unit in a run-down row house. The previous month, according to a neighbor, Carelli had argued with Leonard Hoskins, another tenant. There was shouting, scuffling, the sounds of a fistfight, and moments later, a bloodied Richard Carelli stumbled from the building, the neighbor says. He thought Carelli had lost the fight, that the blood was his own, so he didn't call the police. Investigators would later discover that the landlord had been trying to evict Carelli and Michele and that Hoskins had been drawn into the dispute.

Hoskins's sister, Ureena, reported him missing, but the authorities didn't do much more than file a report. Three weeks later, she went to San Francisco and started investigating on her own. She was the one who found the neighbor and persuaded the police—finally, on January 24—to interview Carelli. He denied the fight with Hoskins, but the police brought in cadaver dogs, who seemed to indicate there was a body in Carelli's van. Carelli at first gave authorities permission to search it but then, according to police, changed his mind and demanded his keys back. They impounded it instead and, amazingly, let him go. Eight days passed before police searched the van and found Hoskins's body inside. By then, Carelli and Michele had fled to Mexico, the children in tow.

Though the murder and kidnapping made it onto the *America's Most Wanted* website, the official search never amounted to much. Even after a tourist saw the fugitives in San Quintin, 150 miles south of the border, there was no follow-up. The wait was slow agony for the Pauly family.

"I had pretty much given up," Ellen Pauly says, admonishing herself for the thought. "I was just so angry at everyone, all the screwups, no communication between agencies. I thought no one really cared. And then, when you least expect it, here comes this total stranger. And he proves that there is still decency in the world."

* * *

Kellie Spring cried when her husband first told her what he was going to do. But when she saw Viana's picture, she agreed, reluctantly, that yes, he had to go. She asked him only to wait a couple of days before leaving. He needed a plan. He needed supplies. Mostly, he needed to give her a chance to accept what he was about to do.

Spring agreed to wait—and started working the phones. At first he assumed there would be an official search party to join, but after calling law-enforcement officials, it became clear that no one in Mexico was looking for the fugitives or the children. If he went, he'd be on his own.

Next he contacted the Pauly family. Missing-children cases draw attention from all kinds of characters, so he knew he might be seen as some kind of crackpot. Indeed, when he talked to Rob Doubleday, Viana's uncle and the family's spokesman, they'd just heard from self-proclaimed psychics, sure they knew where the children were. Doubleday thanked Spring for his interest but doubted he could help.

Spring made it clear he was going to try anyway. The next day, he had 2,500 posters printed up in Spanish, with *secuestrada* ("kidnapped") in bold letters across the top. He included photos of Viana, Faith, Michele, and Carelli, along with a shot of a white 1996 Mercury Mystique, the last car they'd been seen in.

He packed a flare gun, a machete, and all the food he thought he might need. And then, early Sunday morning, 36 hours after his initial Internet search, as Kellie watched with Addie at her side and Caden in her arms, James Spring drove away.

"I knew it was important to him and I had to let him go," Kellie says now, recalling how frightened she'd been. "But he was looking for people who were suspected of murder, and neither of us knew what they might do to protect themselves."

*   *   *

As Spring drove across the border that Sunday morning, his plan was to plaster posters at every Pemex gas station and police headquarters between Ensenada and San Quintin.

He never doubted he would find the girls. He'd lived in Baja for four years in his 20s. "I know the whole 1,059 miles of it," he says. "I know every place to look, even the ones the Mexican police don't know about."

Driving through tourist towns and fishing villages, places that weren't much more than a collection of shacks, he thought about what it might be like to confront Carelli: Does he know his way around? Does he speak Spanish? Does he have money? Does he have weapons? That night, in San Quintin, he came across a Mercury Mystique, just like the one Carelli had been driving. What are the odds? Spring said to himself, excited that he might have stumbled onto the couple so quickly.

He had the cops check it out, but it wasn't Carelli's car. If the police, skeptical of the American with the posters and the staple gun, had doubted his veracity before, they were really questioning it now. He couldn't afford to cry wolf. "I'm sorry," he told the officers. And then he moved on.

On Monday morning, he headed farther south, to the small village of Santa Marie. A gas station attendant said yes, he'd seen the couple within the past three weeks. An off-duty cop confirmed the sighting. Spring was already closing in. "I can't tell you why, but I woke up that day feeling great," he says. "I felt like something was going to happen."

At a gas station in El Rosario, 36 miles south of San Quintin, he began taping up a poster when an attendant said to him in Spanish, "I have seen this woman."

"When?" Spring asked.

"Three days ago," the man said. "She was asking about a cheap place to eat."

Spring walked 100 yards to a motel he knew to be popular with Americans. Sure enough, two men at the front desk told him, the couple had rented a shack a few doors away. Michele was giving dance lessons to local kids to earn a few pesos. "I could feel the goose bumps forming," Spring says. Carelli and Michele were his.

He drove to the police station, a small cinder-block building on the town square, asked for the *comandante*, and informed him that he had a suspected murderer in his village. The comandante requested help from the state attorney general's office, the Baja equivalent of the Texas Rangers, but they wouldn't get to El Rosario before dusk. Until then, Spring and the comandante would have to wait and hope.

Spring kept the Pauly family informed and told Kellie he was safe. He spoke briefly to a U.S. marshal in San Francisco. "This is a tiny village," Spring warned. "Carelli is going to find out I'm here. And when he learns that, he'll leave. And I have him. He's here. Now."

As the sun began to set, Mexican authorities swarmed the house where Carelli, Michele, and the kids were staying. Spring was ordered to remain at the police station during the actual arrest. "I was pacing the whole time, literally doing laps around the station," he says. The officers—"big guys in five unmarked trucks, with big mustaches, black leather jackets, and AK-17 rifles," according to Spring—made the arrest. Spring listened on the police radio. "I hear the guy kind of giving a play-by-play at the dispatcher desk," he remembers. " 'Okay, they're at the house. One of the cars is circling around. They got 'em!' "

The officers returned to the station five minutes later, Carelli shackled in the back of one pickup truck, Michele and the kids in another. "They pull right up in front of me on this little patio area and yank Carelli out of the truck," Spring recalls. "He looks at me, and you can just see that whatever he had alive in him is gone. He sees a white face and he knows the jig is up."

Viana looked nervous but unharmed as Spring assured her that everything would be all right. He promised to stay with her and Faith until they were reunited with the Paulys. "Whenever something bad happened, like seeing her father shackled in a cell, I'd see Viana's eyes get really wide," Spring says. "I'd talk to her and say, 'I have a little daughter myself. And she thinks she's a princess. Just like you.'"

*   *   *

Gene Pauly was waiting on the U.S. side of the border. He hugged his granddaughters, Viana yelling, "Grandpa, Grandpa!" He did not speak to Carelli or to his daughter—or even look at them—as they were turned over to federal marshals and escorted back to San Francisco, where Carelli awaits trial for murder and Michele for accessory to murder for helping him avoid capture. Both also face child abduction charges.

By Tuesday evening, Viana Carelli was back in her grandmother's arms. Viana told her that she'd been hungry and dirty in Mexico. And whenever she saw a police officer, in real life or on TV, she seemed frightened.

The family decided that caring for a traumatized six-year-old and an infant with special needs was too much for the Paulys. So Rob Doubleday and his wife, Sherry, Michele's sister, took custody of Faith.

James Spring went back to San Diego, to his coat-and-tie job, no longer feeling so restless. On his birthday, his wife threw a big party that was also a fund-raiser for the Polly Klaas Foundation, a missing-children's charity.

The Pauly family has invited Spring to visit the girls in So-quel whenever he wants. They'd like to thank him in person. He appreciates the gesture but has so far declined. "I feel like I've done my bit," Spring says. "In my mind, this was always about the kids. I was never looking for attention or praise. I just wanted to do the right thing."

The Pauly home features new photos of the children, to-gether and happy. Faith is alert and healthy, and although Viana remembers her ordeal and misses her parents, she's full of smiles and hugs most of the time. "That little girl," Gene Pauly says as he watches her skip across the living-room floor. "Ten weeks without her was just too long."

Richard Carelli pleaded guilty to involuntary manslaughter in the San Francisco death of his roommate in 2011 and was sen-tenced to six years in prison. As part of the plea deal, charges against Michele Pinkerton for being an accessory to the crime were dropped. Pinkerton pleaded guilty to child abduction and passing a bad check in 2010 and was sentenced to three years in prison. Carelli and Pinkerton have served their sentences and are no longer incarcerated.

KILLER CHARM

by Michael Capuzzo
from the book *The Murder Room*

Alarmed by the growing number of unsolved murders, a group of the world's foremost crime solvers banded together in 1990 to crack cold cases. They called themselves the Vidocq Society, after a legendary 19th-century French detective, and gathered monthly in Philadelphia—where they still meet to this day.

Here, one of their many success stories.

The red light was blinking on the telephone in Richard Walter's hotel room. Who wants me now? he thought. Walter had just flown in from business in London for a meeting of the Vidocq Society, but right now, he was planning to go to the bar. The only five words he wanted to hear for the rest of the night were "What will it be, sir?"

Reluctantly, he picked up the phone. The message was from Vidocq cofounder Bill Fleisher, welcoming him to town—and asking a favor.

"Richard, would you call Jim Dunn? He's a bereaved father whose son disappeared a year ago in West Texas; the cops haven't made any progress. This case has your name on it."

With a groan, Walter dialed the number Fleisher had left. *My sense of duty is inviolable. It's damn annoying at times.*

Duty told him to let the phone ring five times, no more. On the third ring, Jim Dunn picked up.

Walter introduced himself. "I'm a psychologist, Mr. Dunn, whose expertise lies in profiling killers. From the little Bill Fleisher has told me, I suspect my skills might be of some use to you."

*   *   *

At eight o'clock the next morning, Richard Walter and Jim Dunn sat in Walter's hotel room, enveloped in cigarette smoke. The profiler sat erect in a Queen Anne chair, a picture of stillness with his eyes closed. Dunn, a tall man with a craggy face, faced him on a matching Queen Anne. On the table between them, Dunn had piled notebooks, tapes, and newspaper clippings.

Walter opened his eyes and arched his brow. "It sounds like you're hurting, Jim," he said. "How may I help you?"

Walter had spotted Dunn in the lobby at 20 paces. The man's elegant suit, shiny wing tips, and silver hair bespoke the mature, prosperous gentleman of the telephone call the night before. Yet it was the sadness of the eyes that made Walter certain.

Now Dunn explained that he had been working late one Sunday evening in his Bucks County, Pennsylvania, home when the phone rang. He'd thought, It must be Scott. The Sunday calls from his 24-year-old son were a father's joy. After some troubled years, Scott had moved to Lubbock, Texas, where his father had been raised. Scott wanted to make a new life for himself and had recently told his dad that at Thanksgiving, he'd be bringing home a young woman named Jessica*—a

---

*Name changed to protect privacy.

bright, lovely Mississippi State University student who would soon be his fiancée.

But the flat, cold voice on the line was someone Dunn had never heard of. Her name was Leisha Hamilton, and she was Scott's live-in girlfriend, she said. She'd found Dunn's name on a telephone bill. Scott had been missing for four days, and she was concerned.

Dunn was confused. "The only girl Scott ever told me about was Jessica."

Scott had suddenly moved out, Leisha said. He'd taken all his clothes, and even the bed they shared was gone. The only thing he'd left was his car, still parked at the office. When Dunn heard that, he felt a chill. "I knew then something was really wrong," Dunn told the profiler. "Scott would never go anywhere without his car."

When Leisha called again, Dunn recorded her. Now Walter asked to hear the tape. "She sounds so cold," Dunn said as the atonal voice filled the room. "I've never heard anything like it."

At first, the police regarded Scott's disappearance as a missing persons case, but when Scott hadn't turned up after two weeks, Dunn flew to Lubbock to push the investigation. The police had run a Luminol test in Scott and Leisha's emptied bedroom. Luminol detects blood as diluted at one part per million. When the chemical is sprayed on the walls in darkness, any trace of blood—even after rigorous cleaning— would interact with it and glow with a blue luminescence for 30 seconds.

The walls and ceiling glowed as if they had been painted blue. Huge waves and spikes of blood splashed halfway up the wall. DNA tests showed it was Scott's blood.

Dunn's voice broke as he showed Walter the test photos. Scott had died in that room, Dunn was convinced.

Police, too, believed they had a murder on their hands. But they couldn't find a body. They'd combed the prairie with cadaver dogs and helicopters, turned over half the city dump, and even brought in psychics. "In Texas, the state can't successfully bring murder charges without a body or body part," Dunn recalls the DA saying. "You don't have a case."

The police thought Leisha wasn't completely forthcoming, but they figured she was scared, and they hoped to coax her into greater trust.

Dunn took her out to dinner, trying to form an alliance. After that, Leisha kept calling. One day she'd say she loved Scott and was doing all she could to find him. The next day, she'd sound vague and distant, hinting that she might know where Scott's body was but that Dunn would never find him. She also said that since she'd been the closest person to Scott, it was only fair that she get his car. She kept pressing Dunn to give her the keys.

Walter, sitting in the Queen Anne chair, had said nothing for almost three hours as Dunn talked. Dunn's voice cracked. "Well, Mr. Walter, what do you think I should do?"

Walter stubbed out his cigarette and stared hard at Dunn. "Jim, aren't you tired of being the grieving father?"

Dunn's mouth fell open. "I . . . I thought that was what I was supposed to be."

Walter shook his head. His jaw was clenched. "No! You're supposed to be mad! That woman murdered your son! Let's go get her!"

* * *

"Super Sleuth Called to Shed Light on Bizarre Disappearance," touted the front-page story about Richard Walter's arrival in Lubbock.

At eight o'clock in the morning on a December day in 1992, Walter sat down with a police corporal, sergeant, and detective. Walter got right to his point: They should go to District Attorney Travis Ware and press for murder charges against Leisha Hamilton and her former neighbor Tim Smith, a man Walter believed had been her lover and accomplice. Cpl. George White and Sgt. Randy McGuire took a long look at the profiler. The case had been a top priority for over a year. Jim Dunn was a hometown boy, a distinguished alumnus of Texas Tech; his college roommate W. R. Collier, now president of the largest locally owned bank in Lubbock, was still his best friend. There was great public interest in the case, and the police had invested thousands of man-hours. They wanted nothing more than to solve it. But while they liked Walter—and he, them—they weren't convinced the slender, charming Leisha had orchestrated a cold-blooded murder, and they were stymied by the absence of a body and motive.

Walter tried to convince them. "Sometimes, gentlemen," he said, "what's missing is more important than what's present." He held up the photograph of bloodstains revealed by Luminol. "The careful cleanup speaks to an elaborate plot. The murder was purposeful, not recreational."

At the word *recreational*, eyebrows rose, and he explained: "A Ted Bundy type who chose a random victim for sadistic pleasure would have left a far messier, more symbolic crime scene. So the killers knew Scott." He let that sink in for a moment. "The carefully organized crime, cleanup, and disposal of the body point to a power assertive, or PA, killer," he went on. "It's a type I've dealt with many, many times. The killing is all about power—incapacitate, restrain, torture, kill, throw away, 'I win, you lose' kind of power."

He asked them to examine Scott and Leisha's relationship.

Scott was a ladies' man, handsome, bright, and cocky. Leisha, 29, was also very bright, sexy, flippant, and manipulative. "Leisha had a long list of lovers, husbands, one-night stands, wanted and unwanted children," Walter continued. "She had five children by different fathers." His voice took on a sarcastic edge. "She told police she only loved the ones conceived in love." He paused to let that take root. "Leisha would have seen Scott as a challenging conquest and a link to his father's wealth. But like a lot of 24-year-old men, Scott had found someone to take to bed, not home to meet Mom and Dad. When he met a 'decent' girl, it was time to dump Leisha Hamilton."

The day Jessica called and Leisha answered the phone, Scott's fate was sealed, Walter speculated. "If anything is going to get you killed, it's to reject the psychopath and say, 'I'm better than you are.'"

Scott had worked at a stereo shop, and Walter believed the sequence of events leading to his murder began with a raucous Monday-night party at his boss's house. Scott arrived with a tall, gorgeous blonde, who turned out to be a transvestite. According to Leisha, Scott had become seriously ill with the flu during the party—a claim that Walter found suspicious. Scott had slept on the sofa at the party house, and the next evening, Leisha showed up and took him home. A neighbor saw Leisha leading the weak, stumbling young man into the apartment. Leisha said she'd gone out Wednesday to get soup and a thermometer. When a coworker came by the next morning to pick him up for work, the blinds were drawn, and nobody answered the door. Scott was never seen again. Walter believed that it was a simple enough matter for Leisha to call on neighbor Tim Smith to help with the murder. Smith had flooded her with fawning love letters that included "If only Scott wasn't around, we could be together." Duct tape used to patch the blood-soaked carpet that had been cut away and replaced in the killing room had been linked to a roll in Smith's apartment.

"This is a classic setup for a female PA killer," Walter said. "She'll enlist trickery to disable a stronger male and/or acquire a sympathetic and weak accomplice. Leisha did both."

Calling attention to herself was Leisha's big mistake, Walter said. "How do we find out about the crime? Leisha calls Jim Dunn. She knows Jim's going to look for Scott. She's already done in the son; now she wants to do in the father too. She tried to be coquettish with the detectives, calling them all the time with new information, pretending to be afraid of Tim Smith. She moved in with Smith so she could continue to set up her dupe to take the fall. The need for stimulation is quite insatiable for a psychopath, the ego gratification to prove they're smarter than anyone, the gotcha."

Tim Smith missed work the day of the murder, Walter said, and Leisha Hamilton can't account for her activities that day, although her memory is extraordinary for the days around it.

The murder itself was a monstrous affair, Walter continued. He believed Scott was poisoned, imprisoned, restrained, and tortured for two days before his death.

Detective Tal English shook his head sadly. The young detective was persuaded by Walter's profile of Leisha Hamilton as a psychopath, but the others still had doubts.

"They were Texas polite," Walter said. But the whole thing involved too much conjecture for them. And they were convinced they'd get nowhere with the DA, Travis Ware. As Sergeant McGuire told Dunn, "I have seen Ware cut people right off at the knees when he feels they don't have a strong case."

Walter wasn't listening. He was ready to see the DA. "Let's go," he said.

*   *   *

District Attorney Travis Ware, six-foot-one, dark-haired, and impeccably attired, rose from his leather chair behind a huge wooden desk. "Well, you've asked for this meeting," he said brusquely. "What do you want?"

Walter snapped back, "We want charges filed against Leisha Hamilton and Tim Smith in the murder of Scott Dunn."

"You don't have a body or a part of one," the DA said. Without either, they could not meet the standards of corpus dilecti.

The profiler removed his horn-rims and glared. "If you want a body, I'll give you one. It's right here, in Dr. Shepherd's report." He dropped on the desk a slim, blue-bound report titled "Forensic Pathology and Analysis of the Crime Scene in the Murder of Roger Scott Dunn."

"What the hell are you talking about?"

"It's right here," Walter said. "Dr. Shepherd's report proves that Scott Dunn was murdered."

Walter had asked Detective English to have a forensic pathologist examine the crime scene to determine if enough blood had been spilled to indisputably have caused the death of a six-foot-two, 170-pound man. Dr. Sparks Veasey, the Lubbock County pathologist, had refused the job, saying there wasn't enough information to reach a conclusion. At Walter's direction, English had mailed a large package with copies of the entire case file, photographs, and bloody carpet samples to Walter's friend Dr. Richard Shepherd, an internationally known consultant to Scotland Yard. "Dick's brilliance is unsurpassed," Walter said. "And he owes me a favor."

As DNA testing indicated, the blood was 958,680 times more likely to originate from the offspring of James Dunn than from anyone else on earth. Dr. Shepherd concluded that bloodstains in the room: "(1) have not resulted from a natural disease process; (2) are entirely consistent with the infliction of multiple blows from a blunt instrument or instruments; (3) are entirely consistent with those blows being delivered with a force of sufficient strength to cause death; (4) [and] that a child of James Dunn has suffered severe multiple blunt trauma injuries while in the corner of the south and east aspects of this room, and these injuries resulted in the death of that individual." The report was signed "Richard Thorley Shepherd, B.SC., M.B., B.S., M.R.C.C. PATH, D.M.J., senior lecturer and honorary consultant in forensic medicine. United Medical Schools of Guy's and St. Thomas's, Guy's Hospital, London."

The DA looked up from the report, his chin set in defiance. He said, "I'm not sure what Texas law would say about this."

"I just happen to have that section of Texas law with me," Walter said, grinning.

Ware issued a wan smile. "I thought you might."

Walter opened a statute book and read, interpreting as he went. "In essence, Texas law says we have to have A) a body, B) part of a body, or C) a confession with corroborative evidence. We have B. We have blood; blood is connective tissue, which is a part of the body."

Ware leaned back in his chair, tenting his fingers. "All right," he said. "You've got a murder case."

*　*　*

Detective English drove the unmarked car through the breezy Texas spring morning, with Richard Walter smoking in the passenger seat. They pulled into the parking lot of The Kettle, a popular lunch spot. They were thinking takeout.

One Leisha Hamilton, to go.

The tall, dark-haired waitress saw the detective and

scowled. English said, "Leisha, let's go outside and avoid a scene." She nodded and quietly followed him out to the car. "It's time for a little chat," he said.

Four months had passed since his meeting with Ware, and Walter was frustrated by the case's lack of progress. In April 1993, he returned to Lubbock, determined to sell the detectives once more on his idea that Leisha Hamilton was the primary suspect, but nobody was buying. He'd muttered under his breath, "Gentlemen, you have no idea what you're dealing with," and then turned to Detective English. "Young man, take me to the psychopath."

They all exchanged small talk as Leisha got in the backseat. The death stare she'd leveled at English in the restaurant was gone. She was smiling, was chatty, and flipped her dark hair back off her forehead.

"I wish you would explain something to me," Walter said. "I don't know anybody else in America who does a murder and then cleans up the crime scene afterward. That is, unless it is done in their own home. And in this case, you're the only one who had access to that house. And you don't have an alibi."

"But I do have an alibi," she protested.

"You mean you know when he died? Only the killer knows when he died."

"I know when I found out he was missing—"

"Scott Dunn is not missing," Walter sharply interrupted. "He was murdered. We've got that established, and you're a suspect."

The eyes and voice now went as flat as a prairie and held there, unshakable. "Then I guess I don't have an alibi."

Walter appeared to be lost in contemplation, then stared balefully over his horn-rims. "Leisha, I've noticed you seem to have a great ability to attract men. Now, granted I'm old, I'm ugly, I'm tired. But for the life of me, I can't figure out what they see in you. Can you explain it for me?"

A startled silence filled the car. She smiled awkwardly. "Well, I don't know. I've got to get back to work." She opened the door, and she was gone.

English sat stunned. "Richard," he said. "Am I mistaken, or did you just call her a dog?"

Walter grinned. "I thought I did."

"But why?"

Walter lit a Kool. "Leisha thinks she is smart enough to outwit everybody. What we must do is make her feel insignificant—unimportant. This will drive her crazy, and she may well make a mistake."

*　*　*

In January 1995, Walter opened a package from Detective English. Out fell a single piece of white paper on which was drawn what Walter called "quite intriguing original art."

It was a pencil sketch by Leisha of the murder scene— a crude, childlike drawing that documented the torture of Scott Dunn.

Walter phoned English. "Where'd you get this?" the profiler asked.

"An ex-boyfriend she took up with after Scott by the name of Karl Young.* He gave it to me in a coffee shop, looking nervously over his shoulder the whole time."

The drawing indicated that Leisha had chained Scott to a pallet where their bed had once been located. At the bottom of the picture was a legend or key depicting handcuffs, a needle, a knife, and a gun; also depicted were fists and a blunt

---

*Name changed to protect privacy.

instrument. This was consistent with the report of a coroner and blood-spatter expert who'd determined, by the angle of three drops of blood on a far wall, that Scott had died from three lethal blows to the head.

"This is a classic," Walter added. "She drew this to memorialize her achievement." Leisha had made dramatic changes in her life that were also classic post-murder behavior. Few cops understood how killers used murder to stimulate personal growth. It was a very dark self-help movement—"I'm Okay, You're Dead." Since murdering Scott, Leisha had dropped Tim Smith and taken up with Young, a local restaurant cook, with whom she'd had a child. She had also attended nursing school, while continuing to work as a waitress, and graduated at the top of her class.

"Her success doesn't surprise me," Walter told English. "I always said she was extremely intelligent—psychopathically bright and charming. But the nursing school is really quite rich. If you're accused of being a murderess, how do you cleanse yourself of all suspicion? You become a healer and dress in white."

*   *   *

On Friday, May 16, 1997, Richard Walter sat in the Lubbock County Courthouse, anxiously waiting with Jim Dunn and his wife, for justice to be served, at last.

Judge William R. Shaver, his square jaw and graying hair set off smartly by his black robes, had asked Leisha to stand to receive the jury's verdict.

She appeared confident and at ease in a conservative blue dress. According to testimony during the four-day trial, she had told an ex-lover, "There's no way I can be convicted, because there's not a body and there's not a weapon."

Jim Dunn wore his best dark suit and tie. His wife clutched Jim's hand. It was six years to the day since Scott had gone missing.

At the state's table, Rusty Ladd, an assistant district attorney who always wore cowboy boots, nervously leaned forward. The case had been a prosecutor's nightmare. The first grand jury hadn't found sufficient evidence to indict for murder; the district attorney who'd brought the case was bounced out in an election; the new DA had a conflict of interest—his old law partner had once represented Tim Smith. So the DA reached out to Ladd in another county to be special prosecutor. A new grand jury labored over the case, and Ladd wrestled for eight months to get it to trial without a body. In a blow to the case, Walter had not been allowed to testify. Judge Shaver had ruled that a profile of an accused murderer was speculative and not worthy of his court.

In the third row, Walter was still quietly fuming over the slight.

The judge unfolded the paper the jury foreman had handed to him, cleared his throat, and read, his voice booming: "We, the jury, find from the evidence, beyond a reasonable doubt, the defendant is guilty of the offense of murder as charged in the indictment."

Murmurs swept the courtroom. The Dunns turned and looked at each other for a long moment; then Jim threw his arms around his wife and held on, tears streaming down his face. Walter was thrilled to see husband and wife, now his good friends, emerge from a long darkness into light with one swift embrace.

Leisha Hamilton was sentenced to 20 years in prison for the murder of Roger Scott Dunn; she will be released in 2017. Tim Smith was also convicted of first-degree murder but received only a ten-year sentence; it was probated, and he didn't serve time. Scott Dunn's body has never been found.

Leisha Hamilton was released on parole in 2016, followed by one year of probation. She got married in 2010 while still in prison and now lives in Texas with her husband.

Scott Dunn's remains were found in 2016, buried in a shallow grave near the apartment where he was killed.

PARTNERS IN CRIME

by Max Alexander

For winter recreation, it doesn't get much better than Mt. Bachelor, with its 3,365-foot vertical drop and 350 annual inches of snow. The Oregon ski resort has it all when you throw in some kick-off-your-shoes nightlife; the area's Upper Castle Keep Lounge warns, "Choose one of our other facilities if you can't handle too much fun!"

But too much fun wasn't a problem for good-looking Brent Wilson "Wil" Hicks and his athletic girlfriend, Alex Santini. The couple pulled into nearby Bend in December 1998, anticipating a fast-paced season of snowboarding and partying. An Internet stock trader, Hicks could work anywhere that had a high-speed connection for his laptop. After renting a two-month condo, paying $1,800 cash for ski passes and joining the local Gold's Gym, Hicks and Santini settled into a daily routine of a little work, and a lot of play.

At night in the Lounge, the couple made friends with Carey Black, a cocktail waitress, who didn't know that Hicks, whose real name was Craig Pritchert, was in fact a career criminal and a wanted man. At age 37, he'd already done time for bank robbery. Santini was Nova Guthrie, a 25-year-old college grad with no criminal record but a taste for high living. Over 16 months from 1997 to 1999, authorities now say, Craig, often with Nova's help, pulled off precision, armed "takedown" heists in banks

from Oregon to Texas, netting as much as half a million dollars. The robberies earned them comparisons to Bonnie and
Clyde, the bank-robbing lovers who eluded cops for four years
before perishing in a rain of police bullets in 1934.

Shortly after arriving in Bend, Craig and Nova began checking out the Klamath First Federal Bank. It was the kind of bank
Craig liked: in a small town without a lot of cops and across
from a busy shopping center, where a getaway car could blend
in quickly. Best of all, it was open until six on Fridays—after
dark during winter.

On a Friday in late February, Nova was behind the wheel
of a silver Subaru that pulled into the parking lot of the Tim-
bers Bar & Grill, just down the street from the bank. It was
just before six, and as darkness settled in, authorities allege
that Craig donned a latex mask-and-wig likeness of a bearded
old man. He grabbed a walkie-talkie and a white canvas bag,
zipped up his ski parka and headed for the bank. Nova stayed
in the car with the other walkie-talkie and a police scanner.
Her job was to listen for the words "211 in progress"—cop code
for a bank robbery—then alert Craig.

But Craig didn't give the bank's three employees time to
trip silent police alarms. He burst in wielding a semiautomatic
handgun and ordered manager Bill Olsen to lock the door. "At
first I thought it was a joke," says Olsen, "but he got my attention when he cocked the gun and threatened to blow my
head off." This was not the Craig who charmed waitresses and
swapped stock tips at the bar. "Every other word was an ob-
scenity," Olsen recalls. "He knew how to terrorize."

Craig told the operations officer, Rhonda Dent, to draw the
shade over the drive-up window and open the vault. As Dent
filled a bank bag, Craig ordered Olsen and teller Laurie Morin
to their knees, and bound their hands and ankles with plastic

flex ties. When Dent couldn't cram any more bills into the bank bag, Craig whipped out another and demanded she fill that one too. Then he tied up Dent, grabbed both bags and bolted out a side door. It was over almost as soon as it began.

Back in their condo, Craig and Nova counted $120,000 in cash. It was a stunning haul, but their day's work wasn't done. Craig lit the woodstove and tossed in the mask, the remaining flex ties and his ski jacket. On Saturday, he got rid of the radios. On Sunday, in what seemed an amazingly generous gesture, the couple gave Carey Black, their friendly cocktail waitress, the title to their silver Subaru. Then they disappeared in a BMW.

* * *

Even before he met Nova, Craig had been eluding cops, and baffling those close to him, for years. Raised in a middle-class, Catholic family in Scottsdale, Arizona, Craig stood out from the crowd—and not just because he was handsome and gregarious. He was a gifted outfielder and switch-hitter at Coronado High School; the team won the state baseball championship in his senior year. There he met his future wife, Laurie, a pretty blond cheerleader and the homecoming queen. "He said all the right things," recalls Laurie. "You felt like he knew so much."

After graduating, Craig played in a summer league with future batting champ Mark McGwire; at Arizona State University in 1982 (a year after he and Laurie married), he landed on a dream team with Barry Bonds and other soon-to-be major-leaguers. With Craig on track to be a high draft pick for the majors, he and Laurie settled down to raise a family, ultimately having three kids.

But Craig couldn't keep his eye on the ball, so to speak.

Frustrated with sitting on the bench as Bonds and other heavyweights took the field, he dropped out of ASU after one year. He could have transferred to another Division I school or simply cooled his heels, waiting for Bonds to move on. "He had no patience," says Laurie.

Beneath Craig's charismatic exterior was a controlling, manipulative person who craved danger. Unbeknownst to his wife, he had been living a life of petty crime and deception for years. "He gets off on it," says Laurie. "I found out that in high school he was stealing tires off cars at fancy dealerships, and then selling them at a swap meet the next day."

Tire theft escalated to more daring crimes during the late '80s, when the couple separated, in part because of what Laurie says was Craig's repeated infidelity. He seemed to enjoy taunting her, at one point frolicking in the hot tub of her apartment complex with another woman. While she worked full-time as a bank teller to support her kids, her estranged husband was robbing banks to support his taste for the good life. Laurie once spotted him driving a silver Porsche Carrera.

The couple divorced in 1990, and later that year the FBI caught up with Craig in Honolulu, where he'd relocated with a girlfriend. Arrested and convicted of robbing a Las Vegas bank in April of that year, Craig served five years in Arizona's Black Canyon federal penitentiary. There he read the *Wall Street Journal* every day and dreamed of making a fast buck as a day trader when he got out.

After his 1996 release, during a visit with his kids, he told Laurie's second husband, John Pulzato, that robbery was like a drug—and it was his drug of choice. "There is no better high," Craig said, describing how he would sit in his car before a heist and pump himself up, like an athlete getting ready for the big game.

Clearly, he hadn't put crime behind him, which became evident soon enough. On August 12, 1997, investigators say, Craig held up a Scottsdale Norwest Bank. That same day, Laurie was working as a teller at a Norwest branch in nearby Mesa. She believes his choice of banks was no coincidence.

That afternoon, local cops came close to nabbing their man during a spectacular getaway that included a diversionary car fire and a cat-and-mouse chase through a luxury shopping mall, with Craig buying—and changing—clothes several times. In the end, the cops found Craig's car, strewn with wads of cash and a bank money-tracking device—but no Craig. A few weeks later, the bank robber walked into a restaurant in Farmington, New Mexico, and met Nova.

She was a dark-haired beauty from the tiny rural town of Boone, Colorado. Her steelworker dad and schoolteacher mom were strict Christian fundamentalists, and Nova showed little sign of straying from the flock. A member of the National Honor Society as well as the Christian Student Fellowship in high school, she went on to earn a premed degree from Morningside College in Iowa. "She was very intelligent," says her college roommate, Tina Laskie. Laskie says Nova attended church on campus, but also had a bit of a wild side. "She wasn't afraid to get dirty, and she didn't let anybody push her around."

* * *

But why did she throw it all away for a life of crime? Family members can offer little more than sighs of disbelief. Was it true love? Perhaps, but people who know Craig believe Nova was swept up by his forceful personality. "He could sell ice to Eskimos," says John Pulzato.

When she met Craig, Nova was helping her brother Gerald sell vacuum-cleaning supplies in New Mexico. Although Craig

was 12 years older, she once said she saw something in him
that matched something in her. For his part, Craig has said he
had never met any woman like her.

Craig had a reputation as a ladies' man, but as far as cops
knew, he had always kept his love life and his crime life separate. Yet Nova became Craig's perfect partner in love—and
crime.

Their spree began on Halloween 1997 when cops say
Craig and Nova, along with an accomplice still at large, held
up a Bank of the Southwest branch in Durango, Colorado—
cleaning the vault out of $60,000. They avoided big cities, hit-
ting one-horse towns like Aztec, New Mexico. Nova would
case a bank by going in for a money order, then studying the
layout. And Craig figured out you could dunk stolen loot in a
bucket of water (which Nova kept in the getaway car) to disable tracking devices. "I consider Craig one of the more intelligent bank robbers," says Tom Van Meter, a robbery detective
with the Scottsdale Police Department.

But he was an even better fugitive. Using a host of fake
names, bogus IDs and unstoppable charm, Craig and Nova
managed to hide in plain sight—from the slopes of Mt. Bachelor to the beaches of Belize. The money dwindled quickly, especially given Craig's appreciation for sharp clothes, watches
and premium liquor. To fund their "permanent vacation," the
pair continued the holdups. Thanks to several appearances on
"America's Most Wanted," Craig and Nova sightings started
flowing in, and FBI agents say they came close to them several
times—just not quite close enough.

Then the cops got a break. On March 8, 1999, about two
weeks after the Bend heist, Nova turned herself in—possibly
following a fight with Craig. "I think I'm wanted," she told a
Baptist minister, who drove her to an FBI office in Denver.

During a four-hour interview with agents, she spilled the story of their life on the lam. Based on the information she gave them about Craig, all charges against her were eventually dropped, and she was allowed to leave.

Bad idea, in hindsight. Nova was staying with a sister in Cheyenne, Wyoming, where she was working in a restaurant. The FBI doesn't know exactly what happened next, but they believe Craig got in touch with Nova through e-mail. He must have done some serious sweet-talking, because on April 3 Nova didn't show up for work, and her sister's truck was missing. The next day, the truck was found abandoned on the interstate, and five days later Craig's BMW (registered to "Brent Hicks") was found at Houston's George Bush Intercontinental Airport. Under the hood was a false battery compartment packed with $3,030 in tens and twenties. At that point the trail went cold. The robberies stopped.

Enter Special Agent Mike Sanborn of the FBI's Fugitive Task Force in Phoenix, a burly ex-Marine with a nose for hard cases. Sanborn studied Nova's FBI interview, searching for clues. The couple often stayed in Super 8 Motels, so he sent photos of the pair to every Super 8 in the country. When Craig's oldest son played in the state high school baseball playoffs, the stadium was swarming with FBI agents and local cops. But Craig never showed. "It was my feeling they weren't in the country anymore," says Sanborn.

The special agent now believes that after Craig and Nova hooked up again, they fled to Belize. There they spent about eight months on the island of Ambergris Caye, a snorkeling and fishing paradise. With robbery money running low, Nova probably worked in a local restaurant, while Craig occupied himself day-trading. Eventually, agents say, Craig and Nova moved farther afield, spending time in London, Athens and

Cyprus. After the September 11 attacks, Sanborn figures, the couple decided it would be too risky to re-enter the United States, given tighter security checks. But where in the world were they?

In July 2003, four years after Nova's disappearance, Sanborn got a tip that the pair was seen at a nightspot in Cape Town, South Africa. The tipster said Nova was working at the Bossa Nova Club under the name Andi Brown. Sanborn thought it was far-fetched at first, "but several things made sense," he recalls. Nova had worked as a waitress before, and often used aliases that were "four-letter names." So he e-mailed the FBI's legal attaché in Pretoria and asked about Cape Town.

"I got a one-sentence response," says Sanborn: "Cape Town is a fugitive haven." In less time than it takes to park at the airport, Sanborn googled a website for the Bossa Nova that included hundreds of photos from theme parties, where costume-clad regulars and employees danced the night away. "I got to about picture 300, and there she was, plain as day."

The photo, labeled "Giorgos & Andi," shows an attractive, dark-haired woman, smiling cheek-to-cheek with club owner Giorgos Karipidis. But Sanborn had never met Nova in person, and he needed to be sure. "I sent the photo to the Denver agents who had interviewed her, and they said, 'Hey, nice picture of Nova. Where'd you get it?'"

Sanborn then assigned undercover agents from the FBI along with South African police to stake out the club. (South Africa has an extradition treaty with the United States.) Andi had an American accent, agents noticed, and a large sunburst tattoo on the small of her back—just like Nova's. But Craig was nowhere to be seen.

Then, Craig—or "Dane," as he was known around the bar— walked in. When he greeted "Andi" warmly, the jig was up.

"The two of them hugged and kissed," says Sanborn, who was directing the stakeout via cell phone from Phoenix, 10,000 miles away.

* * *

Four nights later, South African police arrested Craig and Nova without incident as they were sitting down to a dinner of Chinese takeout in their $325-a-month sparsely furnished apartment in a mixed oceanside neighborhood. Cops found a pile of fake passports in the apartment, but no guns—or wads of cash. "They were living near the poverty level," one of the arresting agents observed.

Bossa Nova owner Karipidis, who says he frequently loaned cash to Craig and Nova, had become close with them during their two-year stay. When he heard they'd been arrested, "I thought it was a joke," he recalls. He says Nova managed the club and had access to his bank codes and accounts. "They could have taken close to half a million dollars," he explains. "It seems obvious to me they came here to change."

They left in handcuffs—after a final embrace that Karipidis arranged through a friend in Immigration.

It was likely their last kiss. Nova, now in custody near Denver, pleaded guilty in May to three robberies and will get a sentence of up to 20 years, but could serve much less. The following month, Craig, while being held in Arizona, also pleaded guilty to three counts of armed robbery, as well as a gun charge. He is looking at 20 to 22½ years behind bars.

Karipidis says Craig and Nova's crime-free life in South Africa should be considered by prosecutors or parole boards. "They're not the same people they were," he says. "And they never hurt anybody."

Laurie Pulzato, who no longer works as a bank teller after

being robbed at gunpoint herself, disagrees. "The mental duress during robbery is extreme," she says. "What flashes through your mind is your kids, and you're just praying, Please don't kill me." She says Craig's real victims are their children, who've spent years being stigmatized in classrooms and on the same baseball diamonds where Craig once shone, because of their father's misdeeds.

It's not too much of a stretch to view Nova as yet another of Craig's victims. "He feels responsible for her," says Karipidis, who spoke to Craig in prison. "He feels he's the one who got her into trouble."

But Nova's mother says blaming Craig is too easy. "Had she served the Lord and not strayed from what she knew," says Delores Guthrie, "this would not have happened."

Nova's brother Gerald puts it another way: "We all follow a path, don't we? He had a life to lead, and she had a choice to follow."

Nova Guthrie was sentenced to ten years in prison and was released on parole in 2012. She is now a personal trainer and yoga instructor in Redmond, Washington.

Craig Pritchert was sentenced to twenty-two and a half years in prison. He is incarcerated in Stafford, Arizona, and is scheduled for release on March 28, 2023.

KILLER CONNECTION

by Ann Rule

It was four in the morning, and I was locked in a house that all-too-closely resembled the mansion behind the Bates Motel in the horror classic *Psycho*. I was alone except for my dog Toby and a coworker, who was on the phone in an adjoining office. Wind and rain whipped the fir boughs until they screeched against the window in front of me, the ragged limbs blotting out the faint yellow of flickering streetlights three stories below. And then a hand touched my shoulder as a shadow lowered over my desk. Toby growled deep in her throat. When I put my hand on her collar to quiet her, I felt the hackles rising on the back of her neck.

Why was she acting in such a bizarre way? I whirled in my chair and smiled as I apologized for my crazy dog. My partner was holding a manila folder out to me.

He half-shook his handsome head. "No hard feelings," he said. "Dogs and I just don't appreciate each other, I guess."

Now I know why. Standing in front of me was a serial killer, a sadist whose days and nights were consumed with murderous obsession. He had killed before and would kill again, many times. I had no idea that a monster hid behind his perfect mask, but my dog—who loved almost everyone—sensed the danger. For once, it was fortunate that I wasn't a man's "type"; I didn't fit the profile of his victims—young, slender, beautiful and a stranger to him. Three decades later, I look back and shudder at the circumstances that threw us together, and how he was only the first of many serial killers who found his way into my life.

*   *   *

"Be careful what you wish for—you just might get it," was an old saw I heard when I was a girl. After reading Truman Capote's *In Cold Blood* at 27, I had one big wish: to one day get inside a psychopathic killer's head and write a book about what I learned. Coming from a family of law enforcement officers, attorneys and social workers, I always wondered why criminals did the things they did. I still wonder today.

The first murderer I met was a woman named Viola who spent months in the two-cell wing of the jail in Mountcalm County, Michigan. My grandfather was the sheriff; Viola was awaiting trial for fatally shooting her husband. She taught me how to crochet and also explained what she called "justifiable homicide." She had bought her husband a new Ford pickup and then surprised him—and herself—when she caught him in it with another woman. Her swift retribution made more sense to me than some of the other homicides I have researched since.

Ten years later, I signed up for every criminology course offered at the University of Washington. When I was only 20, I became a Seattle police officer. Though my degree was in creative writing, my heart was in being a cop. I was eager to listen to both victims and suspects, to discern for myself what was fact and what was fiction. I couldn't imagine a better job, but after 18 months on the force, I had the biggest disappointment of my life when I failed the civil service medical exam because of nearsightedness. At 22, I thought nothing interesting was ever going to happen to me again.

By default, I became a writer. The first lesson in Creative Writing 101 is to write about what you know, and I knew about crime and cops and killers. In the next 14 years I churned out more than a thousand articles about real cases for *True Detective* magazine and its sister publications. Few people were very impressed with my writing credits, but, by then divorced, I was happy to make enough, at $200 an article and $12.50 a photo, to support my five children on my own.

At my editor's request I used a male pen name, Andy Stack. "Who would ever believe a woman knows anything about detective work?" he asked, ending our discussion. I set out to prove him wrong, attending scores of trials and working toward an associate's degree in criminal justice.

In the early years, I didn't formally meet the accused, which was fine with me. Sometimes, though, investigators pleaded with me, saying it would help victims' families to have their stories told, and they made introductions. I found remarkably brave people who had lived through the deepest tragedies and I joined their group: Families and Friends of Victims of Violent Crime.

I soon realized that if I was serious about presenting the psychopathology of murderers, I would have to spend time in jail and prison myself—if only for visiting hours.

In the spring of 1975, after years of rejection slips, I finally landed a contract with a modest advance to write a book about an unidentified serial killer who was still on the loose and was thought to have abducted and murdered at least eight young women in Washington and Oregon. However, my contract stipulated that someone had to be arrested and convicted of the crimes; only then could my book be published.

I knew that on a summer day in 1974, the prime suspect in the case had attempted to lure several girls away from Lake

Sammamish State Park east of Seattle by asking them to help him unload a boat. Tanned and good-looking, he had said his name was Ted, and he wore a full cast on his arm. The girls who refused to go with him lived, but Janice Ott, 23, and Denise Naslund, 19, walked away with "Ted" and never returned.

How would I find out who "Ted" really was? Knowing how self-absorbed serial killers are, and that they often love to read about crime themselves, I thought about putting an ad in the personals column, something provocative enough to convince him to call me. And I put hints in my *True Detective* articles that I was willing to serve as an intermediary with the police.

I need not have bothered. I soon came to realize that I already knew Ted. As unbelievable as it sounds, it was Ted Bundy, the same man my dog didn't trust, who was my partner at the Seattle Crisis Clinic two nights a week for a year. Every Sunday and Tuesday during the all-night shift, we were the only people fielding phone calls from strangers in emotional distress, working side by side in the looming Victorian house that was clinic headquarters. But despite spending 12 to 16 hours a week alone with Ted Bundy, I found out I hadn't really known him at all. It would be three years before I had the first hint about his secret life.

On September 30, 1975, Bundy called me from Salt Lake City, saying he had been arrested and was going to be in a lineup, viewed by a kidnapping victim. "Ann, I'm in a little trouble. You're one of the few people I really trust in Seattle . . ."

Actually, he was in a great deal of trouble. By the time Ted called me, there were not only eight missing women in Washington and Oregon, but at least four in Utah, five in Colorado, and two in Idaho. They had disappeared during a span of 18 months. The actual toll is probably much higher than 19. After he escaped from jail twice and eventually made his way from Glenwood Springs, Colorado, to Pensacola, Florida, the FBI estimated that Ted Bundy had killed a total of at least 36 women.

When presented with that number, he smiled slightly and told Florida detectives, "Add one digit to that, and you'll have it."

Did he mean 37? Or 136? Or 360?

Ted Bundy's name never crossed my mind when I got my book contract, and yet six months later I had to face the possibility that I might be writing about someone I knew. Fortunately, it was a nonfiction book, because the situation was too implausible to sell as a mystery novel: Crime writer discovers her friend is wanted killer. It sounded much too contrived. But that was the way it happened. *The Stranger Beside Me*, about Bundy as I knew him, was published in 1980, and is now in its 50th printing.

Between the time of his final arrest in 1978 and his execution on January 24, 1989, in Starke, Florida, Ted wrote me dozens of letters. He never came right out and admitted his crimes, although he once said, "Ann, I planned my escape for two-and-a-half years. I had my freedom and I lost it through a combination of compulsion and stupidity." Compulsion was the operative word. I don't think he could grasp that as long as he was free to walk the streets, he could not stop killing.

* * *

I continued to write *True Detective* cases for bread-and-butter money—and to pay my mortgage. I was probably the only true-crime writer who had known a serial killer during and after his crimes. I had written a successful book. My wish had come true. But as a result I would never again unquestioningly trust the people I met.

I had dinner twice with an attractive detective who was popular with his fellow investigators and seemed polite and considerate. But there was something menacing about him that I couldn't put into words. Three years later, he was convicted in the shooting death of an ex-convict believed to have been involved with him in a burglary ring.

One of my first editors shook his head when I suggested a book on serial killers. "They're a fad, Ann," he said. "Like Hula-Hoops. Next year, nobody will be interested in them." Right. My next three books were about serial murderers. My crossover book—a term writers use to signify the difference between small sales and outright success—was *Small Sacrifices*, published in 1987. An old friend, the late Pierce Brooks, once a captain in the Los Angeles Police Department and an expert on serial killers, called me in the spring of 1984 from his Oregon home. "Ann," he said, "I can't tell you much, but I'm a consultant on an amazing case here in Eugene. You'd better get down here for the trial before some real writer hears about it—it's your kind of case."

Stung, I protested, "I'm a real writer—"

"You know what I mean," he said. "One of those bestselling writers from New York or Los Angeles may beat you to it. Come down, and I promise you won't be sorry."

So I spent that spring at the bizarre trial of Diane Downs. She was a flamboyant defendant, accused of shooting her three children in the mistaken belief that, if they were out of the picture, her married lover would return to her. Two of her children miraculously survived, and were placed in the foster system.

While caring for children was onerous for her, Diane enjoyed being pregnant. She had even been a surrogate mother, bearing a child for a relative stranger. "You have someone inside, a friend you can talk to," she explained. After the shootings, she deliberately conceived another child to replace the seven-year-old daughter she had killed. Hugely pregnant during her trial, she clearly loved being the focus of attention. It didn't seem to matter to her whether that attention was positive or negative.

A few weeks after her conviction, I visited Diane in the Lane County Jail. We spoke by intercom through a glass barricade, and she was animated and upbeat, becoming more so when a fellow prisoner asked for her autograph. The following morning, Diane gave birth to a baby girl. She graciously let Doug Welch, the detective who had helped convict her of murder, hold her baby. Then the child was placed for adoption.

Over time, we exchanged letters. Diane wrote mostly about how much motherhood meant to her, but avoided answering any of my harder questions. She escaped once and was recaptured, and now, two decades later, she is still incarcerated, in the Valley State Prison for Women in Chowchilla, California. Her surviving children, who were eventually adopted by the prosecuting attorney and his wife, are adults now—and doing well.

*   *   *

After *Small Sacrifices* came out, I began to get hundreds of suggestions from readers for book subjects. Obviously I couldn't look into them all, but there were times when I felt an almost physical tug urging me to help unveil the truth. I remember reading a 1997 story about Sheila Blackthorne Bellush, the young mother of quadruplets who was savagely murdered in her home in Sarasota, Florida. Like anyone else, I was horrified and wondered who could possibly have hated her enough to shoot and stab her in front of her four toddlers. But I was writing another book at the time, so I didn't pursue the case.

Then, in January 2000, I got an e-mail from Kerry Bladorn, Bellush's sister. Unbeknownst to either of us, Kerry lived two miles from my parents' ranch in Oregon. When I called her, she said, "I've been looking for you for so long. If my e-mail hadn't reached you, I was going to give up. From the moment my sister divorced her first husband ten years ago, she believed he would find a way to kill her. Sheila said Allen Blackthorne never let any woman leave him. She knew his other ex-wives were in hiding."

Sheila had warned Kerry that if she died suddenly it wouldn't be the way it looked. Allen was furious because Sheila had taken him to court repeatedly to gain full custody of their two daughters, and also for her share of their financial assets. Tearfully, Kerry had promised her sister that if anything ever happened, she would see that it was investigated. "And then she told me to find Ann Rule," Kerry continued, "and ask you to write a book about her."

I couldn't say no. To research *Every Breath You Take*, I went to San Antonio for multimillionaire Allen Blackthorne's murder trial, and then to Sarasota to talk to sheriff's detectives there.

Blackthorne, the co-owner of a company that sold muscle stimulating devices, was supremely confident throughout his trial. He turned often to mouth "I love you" to his current wife, Maureen, who was sitting beside me. But Blackthorne lost his sangfroid when the jury came back, and he was sentenced to life in a federal prison.

I always spend time where the crimes occurred. In Sarasota, I stood in front of a white house trimmed in yellow, sheltered by lush tropical plantings. I looked at the garage window where Sheila's killer had entered, and silently promised her I would tell the story she no longer could.

That was not the only time I felt I had received a plea from beyond the grave. In 1985 a woman named Linda Bailey Brown was shot to death in her home, a small rambler in Garden Grove, California. That apparently was not the end of Linda, though. A few weeks afterward, her husband, David, told a friend he couldn't sleep in his bedroom any longer. Something kept awakening him and his mistress, the 16-year-old sister of his deceased wife. "There's a ghost there," he insisted. There may have been.

I am barely adequate as a photographer, but I took a picture of the front of that house for *If You Really Loved Me*, the book I wrote about Linda Brown's case. When I picked up the prints, I was startled to see a blond woman staring from the front window. That wouldn't be unusual, except that the family who then occupied the property were Asian, with jet-black hair. And there was only an inch or two of space between the windows and the venetian blinds that covered them. No flesh-and-blood person could stand between the two. Later, when the sun was at the same height and the shadows were identical, I tried to duplicate the photos. I never could.

I visited David Brown in the Orange County Jail after he was convicted of arranging his wife's murder. Despite the overwhelming circumstantial evidence presented at his trial and the testimony of his own daughter, Cinnamon, he was glib as he urged me to reinvestigate the charges against him. "Ask my family," he said. "They'll tell you I'm a nice guy."

But David lost me when he boasted that he'd bought his late wife a funeral plot where "she has a nice view of the fountains." That expense had taken only a small portion of the nearly half-million dollars he collected on Linda's life insurance policy. David Brown paid $330,000 cash for a house for himself in the Anaheim Hills with a much better "view."

*   *   *

As strange as it might seem, I once heard from a killer-in-waiting before he set out to poison his wife. Dr. Anthony Pignataro of Buffalo e-mailed me in 1998 asking if he might call me about an important matter. I provided my office phone number, and he did call—asking me to write a book about the outrageous injustices he said he had suffered at the hands of the New York State Department of Health, which had taken away his medical license. Dr. Pignataro said he was a plastic surgeon. He had never been board-certified in that specialty and his credentials were suspect, although I didn't know it then. At least one young patient had died in his office during surgery, and others came close to death.

Pignataro was a persuasively smooth man with a deep voice, and he even put his wife on the phone with me. I explained that I didn't write medically oriented books; I wrote true crime. Undeterred, Pignataro sent me a rough manuscript he said his wife had written. I glanced through it, and promptly forgot about the Pignataros. I had no way of knowing that the woman who spoke to me on the phone wasn't his wife at all, but rather his mistress.

More than a year later, a reader in Buffalo sent me a newspaper clipping about a woman named Debbie Pignataro who lay near death in a local hospital from some unknown poison. "Pignataro . . . Pignataro . . . ?" Then I remembered the angry doctor. Because I knew he'd read my books—and two of them were about killers who used poison—I sent copies to Frank Sedita, the Erie County prosecutor handling the case. As it turned out, Debbie had been poisoned with arsenic from ant traps.

Most of us have arsenic in our blood—usually from five to ten micrograms per liter, or a little more if we eat shellfish. It's not enough to hurt us. When she was admitted to the hospital, Debbie's blood tests showed she had 29,580 micrograms per liter.

I'm happy to say that she fought her way through crushing pain and paralysis, determined to live for her children. And she made it. And I did write a book about Anthony Pignataro, who will reside in a New York penitentiary until 2019. Needless to say, it was not the ending he had envisioned.

*   *   *

After 23 books, I've become fairly selective about the cases I decide to write about. Some are too old, going back 50 years or more. Killings like those of Jon-Benet Ramsey and Nicole Simpson have already had what I call "saturation coverage," meaning anyone who watches television already knows all the details. And many cases simply lack suspense: He did it, he got caught, he confessed, case closed.

Truly engrossing homicides are those where the solution seems tantalizingly close, and yet detectives are stymied for months—or even years. Along with three separate sheriff's task forces, I waited more than two decades for the denouement of the longest-running serial murder mystery in the Northwest: the Green River Killer homicides, with at least 48 young female victims. From July 1982 to December 2001, my linen closet held no sheets or towels because it was packed with newspaper clippings, maps, audio and videotapes, and my notes about locations and suspects in this baffling series of disappearances, followed by the discovery of their decomposing remains.

Most of the victims, runaways and teenagers who had turned to life on the street for survival, vanished within a few miles of where I lived at the time, in South King County, Washington, practically in the flight path of the Seattle-Tacoma

Airport. Sometimes I stopped to warn girls who stood in the rainy nights along Pacific Highway about the danger there, but they usually assured me they would be fine.

Sadly, many of them were not, and the toll continued to rise. I never felt "hinky"—a cop's term for intuition that something is wrong—about Ted Bundy, but given my proximity to the Green River Killer's stalking ground, early on I developed a feeling that I had probably seen him. I came to believe that at some point I had stood behind him in a supermarket, or sat next to him at a restaurant.

In the first three years of the probe, I fielded several calls a day from people convinced they knew his identity. Most were from women turning in their ex-husbands or ex-boyfriends, and many of them were chillingly convincing. Rumor had it that the killer was a cop, and I was tipped to the names of many detectives I knew, which gave me pause.

My daughter, Leslie Rule, is a writer too, and we often hold book-signing events together. On several occasions she mentioned a man she spotted at our signings. "He never buys a book, Mom," she said. "He just leans against the wall and stares at you."

In 1987, a woman who sold her house to a divorced man in his late 30s called me. The man, who remained a neighbor, had later asked this woman for help removing a bedroom carpet, ruined with spilled "red paint." He matched the composite drawings resulting from Green River witnesses' observations. She and her friend strongly suspected that he might be the killer. I met with them and agreed their suspicions were important enough for me to take them to the task force. Before I did, I drove by his house—which was less than two miles from my own. It was an ordinary little house, two blocks off the Pacific Highway.

I had no idea, of course, that the Green River Task Force was already looking closely at him. But when a search warrant was executed on his property and a meticulous combing of the house netted no physical evidence linking him to the victims, they couldn't proceed.

It would be 15 more years before Gary Ridgway was arrested and charged—initially, with four homicides of young women. Forensic science had progressed to the point where Ridgway's DNA profile could be matched absolutely to body fluids found on some of the victims. In December 2001, his picture flashed across television screens and front pages of newspapers up and down the West Coast.

I didn't recognize him, but my daughter did. Leslie called me and said, "That's him, Mom."

"That's who?"

"The man I told you about—the one who watches you. It was Gary Ridgway!"

I knew she was right two-and-a-half years later as I viewed 105 hours of taped interrogations between Ridgway and the task force detectives. I froze every time I heard Ridgway say my name. Sometimes he spoke of reading my books. He also admitted why he had lied to the police at first, downplaying his cruelty, and the fantasies of torture he had toward all those lost girls.

"I heard a popular Northwest true-crime author was going to write a book about me," Ridgway said. "I wanted to make the best impression possible."

As I wrote *Green River, Running Red*, I sometimes shivered to think that I had any place at all in Ridgway's thought processes. I didn't want to be inside his head or to think of him watching me when I didn't know he was there.

Ridgway has begun serving 48 consecutive life sentences,

isolated in a small concrete cell in Walla Walla, Washington. It's unlikely he will be allowed to read my book. And that's just as well. He wouldn't like it. There is no way for a sociopathic serial killer to make a good impression on anyone. While I do explore his twisted world in my book, my concern is—as always—with the lives of the young women he murdered, lives cut short by a man who is addicted to killing.

Am I afraid? No. When I began writing in the true-crime genre, I made up my mind not to let it frighten me or blunt my life. I don't have nightmares because the sadness and terror goes from my fingertips into my computer. Still, I know that in the future there will undoubtedly be other strange connections to the people I write about. And that's just part of my job, because I truly believe I'm doing what I was meant to do: speaking for victims who can no longer speak for themselves.

Diane Downs was denied parole in 2010 and will be eligible to apply again in 2020. She is currently incarcerated at Central California Women's Facility in Chowchilla, California.

*   *   *

Dr. Anthony Pignataro was released from prison in December 2013 and changed his name to Anthony Haute. He is living in the Miami area and runs a cosmetics company called Tony Haute Cosmetique. He has also sought work as an elder care provider.

*   *   *

Gary Ridgway pleaded guilty to another murder in 2011, so he is now serving forty-nine consecutive sentences. He remains in a small concrete cell in Walla Walla, Washington.

THE ALMOST-PERFECT KIDNAPPING

by Joseph P. Blank

The abduction of ten-year-old Kenneth Young four years ago loomed as one of the few unsolved major kidnapping cases in the FBI's history. His ransom for $250,000 made it then the second-largest payoff in the annals of FBI cases. Yet more than 30 months had passed without a clue being found to the identity of the criminal. And time was on his side: California's three-year statute of limitations on the felony of kidnapping was running out ...

*   *   *

At about midnight on Sunday, April 2, 1967, Arline and Herbert Young returned to their Beverly Hills, California, home after visiting friends. Mr. and Mrs. Young looked in on their four children. All were sleeping soundly, and the Youngs went to bed.

An hour later a car turned quietly into the drive, and a man softly climbed the Youngs' outside steps to the second-floor deck; the sliding glass door to Kenny's room, where he slept alone, was unlocked. The man entered, stepped to the bed and gently but persistently shook Kenny's shoulder. When the startled boy uttered the first squeak of a yell, the intruder hit him four blows on the head and said, "Shut up or I'll kill you."

Quickly, he wrapped adhesive tape across Kenny's mouth and eyes, dropped an envelope on the bed and guided Kenny, dressed only in undershorts and socks, down the steps and into the car.

"All clear?" he whispered into a walkie-talkie.

An accomplice on the corner three houses away replied, "All clear."

About 20 minutes later, the kidnapper parked, led Kenny up a flight of steps and to a bed with a bare mattress. He placed the boy facedown, tied his hands and feet to the bed with wire, and plugged his ears with wax.

*   *   *

Monday morning at the Young house was routine, except that Kenny did not come down for breakfast. At eight, Mrs. Young went upstairs to awaken him. There was the envelope on the empty bed; inside, a typed carbon-copy message. "Do not call the police or your missing merchandise will be vindictively destroyed," it read in part. "Give a reasonable explanation to all interested parties concerning the absence of this merchandise. We need $250,000—in hundreds only—be at the pay phones at the Standard Station, northeast corner of Westwood and Ohio, at 6 p.m. on Wednesday."

Kenny's up to another one of his practical jokes, Mrs. Young thought as she showed the note to her husband. Young went to his son's room and took in the scene: bedding strewn on the floor, and the glass door open. As the truth hit him, he felt a surge of anger, then terrible fear. He turned to his wife and said, "I don't think it's a joke." They looked at each other, embraced and cried for a while. Then, ignoring the warning, Young said, "I'll call the police."

Minutes later, Beverly Hills police arrived, followed shortly by FBI agents. A fastidious check of Kenny's room, the outside staircase and drive produced no clues, no fingerprints. And the letter was too fuzzy to trace the typewriter used to write it. The Youngs were counseled by the FBI agents to follow the kidnapper's instructions to the letter. They would take no direct action until Kenny was safely home.

Although the agents had assured the Youngs that the kidnapper was interested only in the money, not in harming Kenny, time passed excruciatingly slowly for the next two days. The parents avoided speculative talk about Kenny, but each ring of the telephone sent their nerves twanging. "Why Kenny?" they kept asking themselves. "My God, what's happening to him?"

* * *

On Wednesday afternoon Young, chairman and president of the Gibraltar Savings & Loan Association, put up stocks from his own and his father-in-law's resources as collateral, and borrowed 2500 $100 bills. FBI agents briefed him: "We'll have our men spotted throughout the Los Angeles area. Make the conversation as long as possible so we can try to trace the call. Try to remember every detail. Under no conditions will we do anything to jeopardize the safety of your son. Our work begins after his return."

Young reached the Standard station at 5:35 and waited, tensely. At six o'clock the phone rang and a voice ordered: "Go to the corner of Sepulveda and Moraga. There's another Standard station there, with a telephone booth. Good-bye."

At the second station, Young waited an interminable 45 minutes before a 1965 white Chevrolet—license plate NBD770—drove up and its driver motioned Young to follow.

The white Chevrolet stopped in a barren area near the San Diego freeway. Staring at the rearview mirror in the near-darkness, the apprehensive father saw a slim man with wraparound sunglasses step out of the car. Young was struck by the man's walk—"deliberate, easy, self-assured"—and his thick black hair with so perfect a hairline that Young thought might be a wig.

The kidnapper stopped at the doorpost behind Young's left shoulder.

"Hand me the bag," he ordered.

"When will I get my son back?" Young asked.

"Tonight. Go home and wait for a call."

Young handed the money over and said, "God help you if anything happens to my son."

*   *   *

While the frantic father waited for the promised telephone call, Kenny slept in the rear seat of a car in the basement garage of an apartment house. He had been given four sleeping pills before being placed there by the kidnapper sometime after the payoff. At 3 a.m. he awoke groggily, rang the bell of an apartment and told the sleepy occupant, "I've been kidnapped and I'd like to call home."

*   *   *

On April 10, Los Angeles police found the white Chevrolet abandoned in a shopping-center parking lot. It proved to be a stolen car, which the thief had modified with special switches that deactivated the brake lights and overhead interior light. Analysis of dirt vacuumed from the floor revealed earth that contained both freshwater and saltwater diatoms—minute, shell-like particles that are virtually indestructible. In only one place in southern California, scientists told the agents, did the diatoms occur together: the abandoned Grefco Mine laboratory, where earth with freshwater diatoms had been trucked in from out of state. But agents could not attach any significance to this conclusion at the time.

Though the ensuing routine of detective work turned up no definite clue as to the kidnapper's identity, the FBI realized that it was dealing with a criminal who had a law enforcement background. The canyon where the money changed hands was a dead zone for radio transmission, a fact generally known only to law officers. The kidnapper had approached the Young car like a policeman—standing by the doorpost to avoid being struck if the driver suddenly flung open the door. The use of overhead and stoplight turn-off switches was little known outside of law-enforcement agencies (which use them to assure blackout of their cars during nighttime surveillance activities). And not a single ransom bill had surfaced. In questioning and eliminating hundreds of suspects, agents checked out former law officers and private investigators involved in shady or illegal activities, but their efforts were fruitless.

As the months passed, the investigation became a plodding but never-waning game—to keep talking with suspects, alert for the slightest wisp of a clue; to watch for the ransom bills and assume that the kidnapper would remain in crime because he couldn't spend the money for a long time; and to hope that he would make a mistake.

The Youngs moved to another house to help Kenny forget his frightful experience and acquired two large watchdogs. After two years the family retained little hope that either the kidnapper or the money would ever be found.

*   *   *

On September 29, 1969, Eugene Patterson, an ex-convict, was arrested for the armed robbery of a supermarket in Alhambra, and also identified as one of the two men who had held up a theater the previous September. Patterson readily admitted his guilt and named Ronald Lee Miller, a 38-year-old special agent in the Intelligence Division of the Internal Revenue Service, as the planner of the robberies.

When police arrested Miller, a search of his apartment produced more than 14 guns and an extensive array of disguises. Although he calmly and confidently denied all charges, and nothing specifically linked him to the Young case, his alleged criminal involvement and his experience as a law officer fitted the skills of the kidnapper, and FBI agents wanted to know more about him.

They began asking Patterson about his relationship with Miller, urging him to try to reconstruct his activities during late March and early April two years before. He disclaimed any knowledge of the kidnapping. It could never have ended there, but agents intuitively believed he was withholding information. Patiently, almost amiable, they continued talking to him. Finally, on February 12, 1970, Patterson started to tell what he knew about the crime.

He had met Miller in 1962, he said, and subsequently teamed up with him in a number of robberies. Then, early in 1967, Miller talked with him about a kidnapping. His job as an IRS agent gave him access to confidential information about wealthy people, and he displayed a list of names, including Young's. Miller drove Patterson in a government car to the old Grefco Mine and told him it would be the ideal place to hold the kidnap victim. On the night of April 2, Miller and Patterson drove in two cars to Beverly Hills. Miller handed him a walkie-talkie, stationed him on a corner and told him to call a warning if anybody appeared. The following day Miller gave him $1000 in $20's without any explanation.

When Patterson told Miller some weeks later about being questioned by the FBI, Miller replied, "If you involve me, you will be taken care of."

*   *   *

Was Patterson telling the truth? He represented the primary and damning witness against Miller. If evidence supported Patterson, the case could go to a grand jury. With the statute of limitations having less than two months to run, the FBI intensified its investigation.

Miller, who scoffed at the accusations and denied everything, was an unusual personality. An employee of the Internal Revenue Service since 1964, he was considered knowledgeable in surveillance techniques, typewriter evidence and the operations of Swiss banks where money could be deposited under a numbered, secret account. In discussing hypothetical crimes with one colleague, he stated that "hot" cash could be kept away from the law by having it picked up by a courier from a Swiss bank.

Bureau artists altered several photographs, including Miller's, by adding the wraparound sunglasses and straight hairline described by Young. When agents then asked Young if he recognized the kidnapper, he promptly picked Miller's picture. Soon afterward, Patterson's common-law wife revealed that she had picked up an extension phone prior to the kidnapping and briefly heard her husband and Miller discussing the question of "hiding the kid."

Miller denied that he had driven Patterson to the Grefco Mine in a government car. IRS records, however, showed that Miller had use of car 90110, a 1963 Plymouth, between April 3 and 7. The FBI located this car, and lab analysis of scrapings from its wheel wells and the undersides of its fenders proved that the car had indeed been at the Grefco Mine. At 6:55 on the Wednesday evening when the ransom money changed hands, Miller claimed that he was interviewing an automobile dealer on a government matter 30 miles from the barren freeway site. The daily office diary that Miller kept scrupulously verified this, and the dealer confirmed Miller's visit. But in reconstructing the details of that day, he remembered that Miller had actually talked with him in the early or midafternoon, *not* in the evening.

The Los Angeles grand jury heard the evidence against Miller and returned an indictment on March 31, 1970, just four days before the statute of limitations expired. In August he was convicted of the two robberies, and in September he was found guilty of the kidnapping and sentenced to life imprisonment. (His appeal will probably be heard later this year.)

For the FBI, the case remains open until the $250,000 ransom is returned to its owner. If and when Miller is paroled—he will be technically eligible in seven years—agents will be watching for those $100 bills.

Ronald Lee Miller almost pulled off the perfect kidnapping. And if any one word is likely to rasp across his nerves for the rest of his life, it is "almost."

Ronald Lee Miller's appeal was denied in 1978.

HAVEN'T I SEEN YOU SOMEWHERE?

by Tim Hulse

Austin Caballero had been getting away with it for years. A shoplifter who targeted small, high-end shops in London's wealthier districts, he had helped himself to more than £100,000 worth of jewelry and designer clothing over an extended period.

"He was good," says Detective Sergeant Eliot Porritt of the U.K. capital's Metropolitan Police. "I hate using that word for him, but he was well dressed and calm. He would go in and engage the staff in conversation, and as soon as their backs were turned, he'd steal stuff.

Sometimes it wasn't until two or three days later that they'd realize something was missing from the display. Then they'd look on CCTV and call the police. But he'd be long gone by then, so he always had the advantage."

Caballero would probably still be getting away with it were it not for individuals such as Porritt, who is one of a team of so-called "super-recognizers" who have been operating at the Met's headquarters at New Scotland Yard since May 2015 and who in 2016 lent their help to the police in Cologne, Germany.

They sound like characters from a Marvel comic and indeed their talents are close to superhuman, because they have an uncanny ability to remember and recognize faces—even faces that are only partially revealed or highly pixelated.

So when a member of the unit saw a picture of the then unknown Caballero on the Met's computer database of CCTV images of known suspects last summer, he decided to check and see if he had been caught on camera before. It's a matching process the unit calls "face snapping," after the game of snap, in which players look for identical cards.

After a weekend of searching, he'd snapped 10 other images on the database. Eventually, after looking at tens of thousands of images, he would end up with around 40 identifications. It was clear that Caballero was a serious repeat offender.

A media appeal was launched for further information, and in due course Caballero was found and later convicted of 40 offenses of theft and one of racially aggravated assault. He is currently serving three years and nine months in prison.

"Some of these pictures of Caballero went back to 2012," says Porritt, an affable character with a ready smile, who is fiercely proud of the successes of the unit. "He was probably thinking, 'I've committed all these offences and no one's ever come to see me, so I've got away with it.' But that's all changed. We're identifying all these prolific offenders who've gone under the radar for years because no one's ever linked up CCTV images of them."

*   *   *

The beginnings of the super-recognizer unit go back to the serious civil disturbances in London during the summer of 2011. It became clear then that the Met had no systematic way of dealing with large numbers of CCTV images. So the first step was the creation of a computerized database of images that could be searched by various criteria such as ethnic appearance, clothing and hairstyle. When the database was put into use, it became clear that certain officers had an uncanny ability for recognizing faces.

"I first started hearing about super-recognizers in 2011," says Acting Police Sergeant Paul Smith, who developed and now manages the seven-strong unit, plus a network of around 170 other super-recognizers, both officers and civilian staff. "When we started using the database, it became clear that certain officers, like Eliot, were giving repeat identifications—not just one, but four, five, six, and on a regular basis."

Porritt had no idea he had a special talent until Smith contacted him to tell him he was on his super-recognizer list. Now 37, he joined the force in 2008. Growing up in the leafy northwest London suburb of Belsize Park, he'd dreamed of working in the public services and making the world a better place, and it was after a job as a civilian assisting a child abuse investigation that he realized the police force was where he wanted to be.

"I've always been good with names and faces but I was never aware when I was a kid of people going, 'Oh my god, how did you remember that?'" he says, laughing. "It's strange, it's only through working at the super-recognizer unit that I realize people don't see other people the way I do. In the past I'd be looking at two pictures and go, 'That's the same person,' and someone else would say, 'Are you sure?' And I'd go, 'Are you blind?!'

"We super-recognizers can remember faces we've seen years ago. The average person can memorize 20 to 50 percent of faces but academics tell us we can memorize 90 percent."

*   *   *

Between one and two percent of the population has this special skill, and scientists are baffled as to why. However, it can be scientifically tested, and all the members of the super-recognizer unit have been proven to share the ability. And it's paying dividends.

"Since the unit started in May 2015, we've made more than 1,800 identifications," says Porritt. "And that's led to more than 900 completed cases."

Porritt and colleagues regularly attend large-scale events, where they can help to identify known offenders. "A couple of the guys were at the Notting Hill Carnival in London looking at a live feed of TV images and feeding information back," he says. "They could tell there were two gangs next to one another, so they were able to give a warning and avert a serious disturbance."

Ten super-recognizers were also assigned to the high-profile case of Alice Gross, a teenager who went missing in west London in August 2014 and was later found to have been murdered. Their work was crucial in finding her body, which had been concealed by her killer under logs in a river.

"The key breakthrough was when we found a tiny flicker of a headlamp that had been missed by all the officers initially viewing the CCTV images in the area," remembers Porritt. "It was a clue that the main suspect had returned to further conceal the body. The area had already been searched, but as a result of our information there was another search and she was found. From there we built a case."

*   *   *

At the beginning of 2016, Porritt and a colleague went to Cologne to help police investigate a huge number of sexual assaults and thefts mainly thought to have been carried out by North

African refugees during the city's New Year's Eve celebrations. It was the first time the unit had helped a foreign force.

"There were 1,546 crimes that night, including 532 sexual assaults," says Detective Superintendent Thomas Schulte, the German police officer leading the investigation. "It was night-time, so the CCTV quality was very bad. Scotland Yard called us to offer their help. I'd heard about super-recognizers before, so I was interested."

"We were there for two weeks," says Porritt. "They'd al-ready identified three officers who had made a lot of idents and were clearly super-recognizers, so we gave them some training. When we got there, they had pictures of 10 or 20 peo-ple on the wall. When we left, the wall was full of suspects."

"I was surprised by how successful they were," admits Schulte, who says they are now thinking of introducing super-recognizer units in Germany. "We always think about technical solutions, but this shows that the human mind is kind of interesting."

It's a good point. The U.S. military recently purchased 500 pairs of so-called "X6 spy glasses" that enable a user to match a face in real time to one on a computer database. But while facial recognition software has its uses and is becom-ing ever more prevalent in other areas, the super-recognizers demonstrate that, for now at least, the human brain has its advantages.

"Almost every image that we've got a conviction out of would never be picked up by facial recognition software," says Porritt. "That relies on perfect conditions, so I don't think it will be good enough for years. CCTV cameras are usually positioned looking downwards. Angles, lighting, pixelation, facial expressions: all these completely change things, and that's why you always need that human element."

And unlike a machine, super-recognizers never stop working, and find themselves spotting wanted criminals—not to mention celebrities—in off-duty moments.

"We're always on the lookout," says Porritt, who on more than one occasion has also been grateful for the fact that so few people share his ability—as when he found himself late at night waiting for a bus next to someone he had once arrested. "Luckily, he didn't recognize me," he laughs.

Austin Caballero was released after serving a three-year prison sentence.

TWO MILLION REASONS FOR MURDER

by Kenneth Miller

For couples craving solitude, the beach at Guana River State Park is an ideal spot for a late-night tryst. Hidden by thickets of saw palmetto, the ribbon of sand unspools along a lonesome stretch of Route A1A south of Jacksonville, Florida. Entry after sunset is officially forbidden, but intrepid lovers often park on the roadside and follow wooden walkways into the dunes.

Justin Barber, 30, and his wife, April, 27, had done just that on August 17, 2002. They were tipsy and amorous, Justin later recalled, having celebrated their third wedding anniversary with dinner at Carrabba's Italian Grill in Jacksonville, followed by cocktails at a bar. Around 10:30 p.m., as they strolled along the water's edge, April suddenly squeezed Justin's hand. A tall man in a baggy T-shirt was approaching. He waved a pistol and yelled something about cash and car keys. Justin stepped in front of April. The gun went off. He grappled with the stranger. The beach went black.

When Justin came to, he found he'd been shot four times—in both shoulders, under the right nipple and through the left hand. The man was gone. Justin called April's name, then spotted her floating facedown in the surf. There was a .22-caliber hole in her left cheek. He dragged her up the beach

until his strength gave out, then left her and staggered to
the road to flag down passing cars. When none stopped, he
climbed into his Toyota 4Runner, turned on the flashers and
gunned it. Nearly ten miles down the road, a motorist signaled
him to pull over and called 911. As Justin was transferred to a
hospital, police and rescuers searched the beach for April.

Lt. Ben Tanner of the St. Johns County Sheriff's Department found her. "She was lying with her head to the north,
facing the ocean," he says. "She didn't have a pulse."

*   *   *

April's photo is etched into her tombstone; it shows a woman
with a brilliant smile, corn-silk hair and exquisite cheekbones.
But her beauty wasn't just skin-deep. April was a survivor of
family tragedy who poured her energy into helping others,
from her younger siblings to the cancer patients she served
as a radiation therapist. "She put more value on relationships
than most people do," says her best friend, Amber Mitchell, an
Internet entrepreneur in Oklahoma City. "She didn't take life
for granted."

Who would want to snuff out such a vibrant spirit? Justin would tell investigators that he thought the culprit was a
crazed mugger. But a few of those close to April developed
their own theory. They suspected the killer was someone she
knew very well.

*   *   *

April grew up in Hennessey (population 2,024), Oklahoma, an
island of century-old storefronts and modest homes in a sea of
prairie. She stood out as sharply as the local grain elevator: an
A student, thoughtful yet popular, as comfortable at a rodeo
as in biology lab.

During April's senior year of high school, her mother was diagnosed with lung cancer and died after six months of agony. April's father, an oil field worker, was too traumatized to care for the kids. Though other relatives took them in, April became a surrogate mom to her siblings Julie, then nine, and Kendon, one. Still, she kept her grades up and was named her class's salutatorian. She went on to the premed program at Oklahoma State University, then studied radiation therapy at the University of Oklahoma.

In October 1998, Amber Mitchell introduced April to one of her business school classmates—a handsome blond named Justin. The two clicked instantly. April had dated a string of men for whom fidelity was not a strong point; Justin seemed different. He spoke of his Christian values. He had grown up in a town even smaller than Hennessey, herding cattle with his older brother on their parents' 120-acre spread. A quiet and solitary boy, he'd blossomed into a star athlete in high school and graduated as valedictorian. He'd married in college and spent a few years drifting between low-paying jobs. When he met April, however, he was newly divorced and aflame with ambition. "He was among the best and brightest in our class," says Amber. "April was attracted to his drivenness."

April and Justin quickly became engaged; then he moved to Dallas, taking a job as a financial analyst for a wood-products corporation. The two carried on a long-distance romance until August 4, 1999, when they married in a small ceremony in the Bahamas.

They relocated for Justin's job to Douglas, Georgia, where April found work at a hospital. A month later her siblings moved in, and the trouble began. Julie was 15 then, and a rebellious teenager; her behavior infuriated Justin, sparking fights between him and April. At one point, according to several of April's confidants, he threatened to never let April bear his children. Within a year, Julie and Kendon were back in Oklahoma.

By then, some of April's loved ones had begun to see a disturbing pattern. "Justin seemed very into appearances," says April's aunt Patti Parrish, a civil court judge. He tried on his jeans from high school every month and fasted until they fit. He made fun of his overweight mother behind her back, and publicly criticized April's singing voice, her taste in clothing and her weight. He warned her not to embarrass him at his company Christmas party and discouraged her from calling or e-mailing him at work. When his barbs made her cry, he mimicked her sobs. Yet April tolerated Justin's mistreatment.

But in January 2001, when Justin was transferred to Jacksonville, April decided to stay put. "She told me that if they lived together every day, they'd kill each other," Amber says. Justin bought a condo in an upscale neighborhood, and the two saw each other on weekends. Usually it was April who drove the three hours to visit.

She just wasn't ready to give up on Justin. He could be charming, and his criticisms dovetailed with some of her deep insecurities. "She was harder on herself than anyone else," says Amber. "She put up with a lot from her men."

Still, there was always a point at which she drew the line.

*   *   *

The man in the hospital bed was soft-spoken and personable, and seemed eager to help catch his wife's killer. But something about him made Detective Howard "Skip" Cole uneasy. Justin's account of the attack was oddly businesslike. "His body language and demeanor didn't seem appropriate," says Cole, 35, who'd been assigned to lead the investigation.

In the days that followed, Cole's suspicions grew. Justin's story was frustratingly vague, and the details kept changing. The case raised a slew of questions. How did Justin escape with minor wounds—he left the hospital with just his arm in a sling—while his wife was killed with a single shot? Why did he claim she'd been drinking, when her blood-alcohol level measured .000? Why had he left his cell phone at home that night, and why didn't he use April's, in her purse on the passenger-side floor of his car? What made him drive so far in search of help, when there were mansions and gas stations along his route?

Meanwhile, April's friends and relatives were pondering possible answers. Aunt Patti remembered that in the summer of 2001, April had told her Justin wanted them to take out $2 million insurance policies on each other's lives. "She asked if I didn't think it weird that he was pushing for such a large amount," Patti says. "I told her yeah but said I didn't think they would qualify. She called back the next day and said, 'You can't say anything to Justin. He'll be furious if he finds out I told you.'"

Justin found a company that would cover them. Not long afterward, April began to suspect that he was having an affair. She told Amber she'd found an earring in his bedroom, and in July 2002, she discovered he was playing tennis regularly with a rental-car agent named Shannon Kennedy. Despite Justin's admonitions, April e-mailed him at work, asking him to tell her when he was socializing with other women. Justin responded with a sarcastic message listing every female he'd glimpsed that day.

April told her boss, Ramesh Nair, that she was going to confront Justin on their anniversary—August 4. She visited her husband that weekend; when she returned, she told Nair

that she'd threatened to end the marriage, but Justin had denied everything. She seemed agitated. On Friday the 16th, she
drove back to Jacksonville.

The next night, she was dead.

Amber and Patti's first thought was "Justin did it." And Nair
was struck by a memory from a few months earlier: "One day,
out of the blue, April said, 'If anything happens to me, suspect
foul play.' I answered with a joke, and she looked hurt, like,
You're not taking me seriously. Don't forget."

*   *   *

April's body was flown to a mortuary in Hennessey. Justin,
seeming withdrawn, shrugged when asked to make decisions
about the funeral. He asked Patti if she would front for burial
expenses. "What about the $2 million?" she responded. Star-
tled, he said, "Did April tell you?" He told her he thought the
policy had lapsed. Patti did some digging and learned that it
hadn't.

At the funeral, in Hennessey's First Baptist Church, a crowd
of 300 overflowed the pews. Several attendees were struck by
Justin's failure to cry, though he appeared to be trying. The
next day, Patti called Detective Cole. She told him what she
knew and put him in touch with Amber.

During a search of Justin's condo, Cole found the insurance
policy in a filing cabinet. Brought in for questioning, Justin
denied his affair with Shannon Kennedy until he was told she
was in the next room; then he insisted that his marriage had
been generally placid.

Cole knew he was dealing with a liar, but arresting Justin
for murder was another matter. There were no witnesses; no
weapon had been found. Even the motive remained fuzzy. Justin was a rising professional with a base salary in the $70,000s;

his wife earned nearly as much. Living apart from her, he could cheat with relative impunity. Did he kill her—and shoot himself—simply to upgrade his lifestyle a few notches?

Cole and his team traveled to Georgia and Oklahoma to interview people who had known or met Justin and April. They probed the couple's financial records and Justin's computer files. They analyzed bloodstains, ballistics and the abrasions on April's body. By July 2004, they had enough evidence to take Justin into custody, but it took another two years of spadework—and, crucially, advancements in computer forensics—before they were ready to go to trial.

*　*　*

The proceedings began on June 12, 2006, in a pink stucco courthouse in St. Augustine, Florida. Cole took the stand only briefly. Much of what the sleuths had dug up was ruled inadmissible: April's conversations with Nair, for example, and Justin's purchase of a bulletproof chest plate on eBay before the killing. Instead, the case turned on a few stark facts.

First, there were the trysts: Justin, it emerged, had carried on at least five during his three-year marriage. The fling with Shannon Kennedy seemed the most serious. Shortly before the killing, he asked her to travel with him to California; two days afterward, he stopped by her office and demanded to see her. He pursued her for several more weeks before transferring to Portland, Oregon, where he quickly got involved with another woman.

Then there was the money. Unbeknown to his wife, Justin had run up $58,000 in credit card debt, mostly through online stock trading. "The adage is true, even if it's corny," Assistant District Attorney Matt Foxman told the jury. "The defendant has two million reasons to commit this crime."

That took care of motive. As to method, prosecutors argued that Justin had spent a year planning the crime. The most damning evidence came from his laptop. On February 9, 2002, Justin Googled the phrase "medical trauma right chest." On Valentine's Day, he tried "gunshot wound right chest." The prosecutor asked, "What are the odds of somebody researching 'gunshot wound to the right chest,' getting a gunshot wound to the right chest six months later?"

*   *   *

On July 19, Justin googled "Florida divorce" and doubtless discovered that if April dumped him, he could no longer be her beneficiary. And on August 17, an hour before the fatal outing, he downloaded 16 songs. Among them was "Knockin' on Heaven's Door" by Guns N' Roses. Another Guns N' Roses number pinpointed his intentions: "Used to Love Her (But I Had to Kill Her)." Foxman played the track in court. Justin, he said, had been psyching himself up for murder.

Finally, there was the crime-scene evidence. Justin claimed he hauled April from the water after she was shot, carrying her in at least nine different positions. Yet the blood on her face all flowed in one direction, suggesting she had been shot on the walkway and left there to die. Foam at her nose and mouth indicated that she'd suffered a "near-drowning episode" before the shooting.

Foxman laid out his theory: Justin intended to shoot April, load her corpse in the car and drive off in search of "help." The scheme went awry when she tried to run. He held her underwater until she stopped struggling, then dragged her to the walkway, where he shot her and himself. The plan derailed again when his pain kept him from carrying her farther. Justin had to modify his tactics, Foxman said, but his strategy never changed: "He wanted the $2 million, he wanted sympathy for being shot, and he wanted to look like a hero who tried to save his wife. *He wanted it all.*"

*   *   *

Justin's attorney, Robert Willis, gamely offered alternative interpretations for each scrap of evidence. But Justin's behavior in a different courtroom three years earlier may ultimately have swayed the jury as much as any lawyer's arguments.

Midway through the first-degree premeditated murder trial, prosecutors played a video deposition Justin gave in 2003 as part of a civil case concerning insurance proceeds. (Those matters remain unresolved.) On the tape, the plaintiffs' attorney grills Justin on the attack, his affairs, his sex life with April. He claims not to remember some key details but answers even the most disturbing questions with uncanny calm. His mouth is set in a downward curve, and he dabs his eyes once. Otherwise, he shows little emotion. When the lawyer asks him to recall the high points of his marriage, Justin says tersely, "We were in love." Pressed for details, he says, "I don't recall specifically."

He seemed equally unmoved when the jurors of the criminal trial, after 33 hours of deliberation, announced their verdict: guilty. His supporters wept, as did April's mourners. Justin barely blinked, even when the jury recommended the death penalty a week later. (Judge Edward Hedstrom later sentenced him to life without parole, and Willis vowed to appeal.) Such detachment is a classic symptom of sociopathy, says University of Texas psychologist Shari Julian, a well-known expert on the disorder.

"The true mark of a sociopath is that he always wears a mask," Julian observes. Unable to connect emotionally, sociopaths learn to gratify their desires without getting caught. They tend to be intelligent, charismatic and monstrously manipulative.

"He's a very gentle person," says Justin's mother, Linda, who still believes in his innocence. "A good guy."

But Amber Mitchell rejoices that the mask is off at last. "This has been a long, horrible chapter in our lives," she says. "I want the jury to know they got it right."

Justin Barber's appeal of his sentence of life in prison was denied in 2013. He also appealed the insurance company's refusal to pay him the $2 million life insurance proceeds, and that appeal was denied as well.

THE KILLER NEXT DOOR

by Josh Bond
from the book *All These Wonders*

I managed a hotel in Santa Monica for about seven years, as well as the apartment building where I lived, which was across the street. Super-easy commute. It's particularly great when you live in LA.

You meet a lot of interesting people when you manage a building. For example, there was a retired couple who lived in the unit next to mine—the Gaskos. The first time I met the husband, I was in my apartment playing guitar and trying to write a song.

There's a knock on the door, and I open it to find a man in his seventies holding a black case. He tells me that he heard me playing music, and he liked it, which was good, and he thought I could use this black Stetson cowboy hat.

Really nice gesture. I thank him, and he says his name is Charlie.

So fast-forward four years, and I'm taking a nap on my couch. I'd been working for two weeks straight, no days off, on call every night. But this particular Wednesday, I was taking off work early and I was going to see this band, My Morning Jacket, in Hollywood. I was meeting a friend. All planned out.

At 2 p.m. the phone rings, and it's my coworker calling from the office—with the FBI.

Before I know it, I'm on the phone with an FBI agent, and he says, "I need to talk to you about a tenant in your apartment building."

I'm on my couch, so I say, "Can we do this tomorrow?"

He says no. "Where are you? Come here now."

So I get to my office, and I take a seat, and there's a large man wearing a dark T-shirt and jeans. He closes the door and throws a manila folder down on the desk. He opens it and points to a sheet of paper. Across the top is *WANTED*, and underneath is a photo of a man and a woman, with the names *Catherine Greig* and *James J. "Whitey" Bulger*.

The officer asks if these people live in the apartment next to mine. And at first glance, I know the woman is my neighbor, Carol Gasko. Yes, I know these guys. These are my neighbors.

And while I've never heard the name Catherine Greig, the name Whitey Bulger is very familiar. I had heard it many times when I was at Boston University. But I didn't really know anything about him. He was a Jimmy Hoffa–type guy to me, like, "Oh, this guy's missing. He's never gonna be found." It was almost like a joke.

So I'm standing there, and the FBI agent says, "What do you think?"

I say, "What does my face tell you?"

He says, "I need percentages."

I say, "Ninety-nine point five, a hundred percent."

So he gets on his cell phone, and while this is happening, it feels like I'm in a movie after an explosion where the sound just disappears and you're trying to process something that you're not familiar with. You don't know what's going on, and you don't know what's about to happen.

This is an old man who bought me a bike light one time because he was worried about me riding my bike at night without one. And now I'm discovering he's a notorious fugitive.

Another agent, this one in a Hawaiian shirt, quickly appears. The agent in the dark T-shirt says, "We need the spare keys to his apartment. I don't want to have to bust the door down."

I say, "Okay, here are the keys."

The agent in the Hawaiian shirt leaves, and then the other agent says, "Look, this guy's pretty high on the Most Wanted list. We could use your help apprehending him."

My first response is, "I just gave you the keys to his apartment and told you he lives there. So I'm not really sure what else I can do."

He says, "Well, we can't just go to his apartment. We have to make sure he's in there. If it's just her, it doesn't really work for us. So why don't you go knock on the door and see if he's there?"

In the previous months, Carol had been telling people in the building, "Charlie has dementia; he has heart problems." They'd put notes on their door during the day that said, "Don't knock on the door." I knew from talking to him over the years that he slept during the day.

I explain this to the agent, and without skipping a beat, he says, "Well, what are you doing tonight?"

I say, "I'm going to a concert."

He says, "You might want to cancel those plans."

So I call my buddy and tell him, "Look, I don't think I'm going to make the show tonight, and I can't tell you why."

As the original shock is dissipating, I realize I'm going to be with these guys until they have Charlie in cuffs. Then things really kick in. One agent places himself at a window that has a good view of the Gaskos' balcony across the street. The other agent wants to go over to my apartment. I tell him to go through an alley and some side streets so he doesn't walk in front of the apartment building in clear view of Charlie and Carol. I walk through the front entrance and let him in from the back.

The FBI agent says, "They just closed their blinds. Did you tip 'em off?"

"I've been with you the whole time. No, of course not."

We get to my apartment, and I draw him a floor plan of the Gaskos' place. He's throwing ideas around about how to get this guy out of his apartment.

My living room wall shares a wall with Charlie's bedroom, so I'm like, "Uh, you know this guy can hear everything we're saying? Like, he's repeated conversations I've had at night with my friends, asking me why we don't curse or fight as much as he and his friends did in his younger days."

We go into my bedroom, and he comes up with an idea. We're going to break into his storage locker in the garage. We go down to the garage, and the FBI agent goes to get his car; he has some bolt cutters in there.

I'm suddenly pumped up. I'm involved in something. It's like a movie. I'm having fun, almost, at this point. The adrenaline is helping me forget about my relationship with these people over the years. I mean, this is the same man who bought me a Christmas present every year for the four years I'd lived there.

Once the lock is broken, we go back to my apartment, and the agent's telling me, "Okay, this is what's gonna happen. I'm gonna go down, we're gonna get everything set, I'm gonna call you, and you knock on his door and bring him down."

And I'm like, "No. I'm going to go across to my office to call him, and I'm going to tell him to meet me there. Then you guys take care of your business."

I'm in my office, and I'm thinking about this guy, my neighbor, who looked after an old woman on the first floor. Who one year, when I didn't write a thank-you note for a Christmas present he gave me, gave me a box of stationery.

I'm thinking, What did this guy actually *do*?

So I go to Wikipedia, and I'm reading about murders and extortion and gambling.

I get to the bottom, and in one of his last public sightings with one of his Mafia buddies, there's a quote from him: "When I go down, I'm going out with guns blazing."

I start to rethink my involvement in the day's events.

Conveniently, my phone rings, and it's the FBI, and they say, "Make the call."

I start to waver: "Look, man, I just read something about this guy . . . and I don't know about this."

He says, "No, no, no—he'll never know. He'll never know." Which is obviously not true. But I am this close to getting to my concert, so I say, "All right, I'll make the call."

I call the Gaskos, and there is no answer. I am relieved. I am so happy that they didn't answer the phone. I call the agent back, and I say, "Hey, man, sorry. They didn't answer. Going to have to do something else."

He says, "Are you sure you don't want to knock on the door?"

And I'm like, "Look, man, curtains closed, guns blazing. What if he comes to the door with a gun?"

He says, "Just be like, 'Hey, man, what's going on?'"

I'm thinking to myself, Uh, he will shoot me before I finish that one statement.

I tell him I'm not going to do that. But while this is going on, Carol calls back. And so I get on the phone and I explain to her that the storage unit's been broken into. Either I can call the police or Charlie can meet me in the garage and we'll look at it.

So she discusses this with him, and she says, "He'll be down in five minutes."

"All right, great." I hang up and call the FBI. "He's on his way. Do your thing."

Then I walk outside, and Carol walks out on her balcony, which is directly across the street. She looks at me, and then she quickly looks down to the garage, and then she looks back at me. I don't know if she knows, but she looks worried.

She walks back in, and then I get a call from the FBI, and they say, "We got him. Go to your concert."

So I go back across the street to my apartment to change clothes, and the adrenaline—the rush—just hits me. I go downstairs, and as soon as I open the door to the garage, it's like a slow-motion shot—there are two SUVs and a half-dozen FBI agents. And my neighbor, Charlie Gasko, is standing there in cuffs, surrounded by agents, laughing and telling stories.

He almost looks relieved. I see Carol standing a few feet away, also in cuffs. And the magnitude of everything that has happened starts to sink in.

She looks at me, and she says, "Hi, Josh," and I can't speak.

I just meekly wave, and walk to my car, and get on the highway, and call my brother, and say, "You'll never guess what happened to me today."

"What?"

"I helped the FBI arrest the most wanted man in the country."

So a couple of months later, my family's a little worried about me, and my friends are taking bets on how much longer I have to live. I get home one day, and there's a letter in the mail from the Plymouth Correctional Facility. I open it, and I see the same familiar cursive writing and the same "shoot the breeze" dialogue tone that I knew from four years living next to Charlie Gasko.

But in this letter, he's reintroducing himself as Jim Bulger.

And so I write him back, and I say, "Look, you know I had something to do with the day of the arrest, and my family's a little worried. So, uh, you know, just a little note of 'everything's good' would be nice."

He writes back and says, "Look, they had me with or without your help. No worries."

So that made my mom feel better, definitely.

New neighbors eventually moved in, and they seemed like nice people.

But what do I know?

After his capture, Whitey Bulger was tried in Boston and convicted on charges related to 11 murders and other crimes. He was sentenced to two life terms. Bulger was beaten to death shortly after being transferred to a West Virginia prison in 2018.

CREDITS AND ACKNOWLEDGMENTS

"A Killer is Loose," by Joseph P. Blank, *Reader's Digest,* December 1961

"The Spy's Son," by Bryan Denson, copyright © 2011 by Oregonian Publishing Co., *The Oregonian* (May 21–27, 2011); *Reader's Digest*, October 2011

"The Drive of His Life," by Paul Kix, *GQ* (May 1, 2017), copyright © 2017 by Paul Kix, gq.com; *Reader's Digest*, March 2018

"The Intruder," by Andrea Cooper, *Reader's Digest*, October 2002

"I Hunted Down the Woman Who Stole My Life," by Anita Bartholomew, *Reader's Digest*, January 2008

"House of Cards," by John Colapinto, from *Vanity Fair* (February 2016), copyright © 2016 by John Colapinto, vanityfair.com; *Reader's Digest International Edition*, November 2017

"How We Trapped Capone," by Frank J. Wilson, as told to Howard Whitman, condensed from *Collier's,* © 1947, The Crowell-Collier Publishing Co.; *Reader's Digest,* July 1947

"The Man Who Rigged the Lottery," by Reid Forgrave, *New York Times Magazine* (May 3, 2018), copyright © 2018 by New York Times Co., nytimes.com; *Reader's Digest* December 2018/ January 2019

"I Stared Down Death," by Christopher W. Davis, *Reader's Digest*, March 2006

"Killer on Call," by Max Alexander, *Reader's Digest*, November 2004

"Heist," by Simon Worrall, *Reader's Digest*, December 2018

"The Almost-Perfect Murder," by Robert F. Howe, *Reader's Digest*, February 2003

"The Killer Among Us," by Max Alexander, *Reader's Digest*, January 2004

"Beth's Been Kidnapped!" by Donald Robinson, *Reader's Digest*, February 1979

"Collared!" by Simon Bouda, *Reader's Digest*, April 2015

"Catching the BTK Killer," originally published as "The Killer Next Door," by Max Alexander, *Reader's Digest*, July 2005

"The Searcher," by Joe Rhodes, *Reader's Digest*, November 2008

"Killer Charm," by Michael Capuzzo, adapted from *The Murder Room: The Heirs of Sherlock Holmes Gather to Solve the World's Most Perplexing Cold Cases*, copyright © 2010 by Michael Capuzzo, published at $26 by Gotham Books, 375 Hudson Street, New York, New York 10014; *Reader's Digest*, August 2010

"Partners in Crime," by Max Alexander, *Reader's Digest*, August 2004

"Killer Connection," by Ann Rule, *Reader's Digest*, October 2004

"The Almost-Perfect Kidnapping," by Joseph P. Blank, *Reader's Digest*, June 1971

"Haven't I Seen You Somewhere?" by Tim Hulse, *Reader's Digest International Edition*, February 2017

"Two Million Reasons for Murder," by Kenneth Miller, *Reader's Digest*, February 2007

"The Killer Next Door," by Josh Bond, adapted from *The Moth Presents All These Wonders: True Stories about Facing the Unknown*, copyright © 2017 by The Moth. Published by Crown Archetype, an imprint of Penguin Random House LLC. "Call Me Charlie" © 2017 by Josh Bond; *Reader's Digest*, May 2017